CONFLICT AND ZEN

Stories of Presence in Heated Moments

Aron C. Viner

Samatva Press

ISBN: 979-8-9995734-4-5

Contents

PART III: Embracing Difficulty

PART IV: Integration and Wisdom

Introduction

Heated Moments

Heated moments arise in the kitchens and living rooms of our lives. We exchange sharp words with partners, children, parents, and friends. These encounters are not fights to be won or transactions to be negotiated. They are dances to be met with care. At their heart, they concern closeness, understanding, and sometimes, the courage to let go.

How do we move through such moments without causing harm? More important than the words we speak is the quality of our presence. To be present is to remain grounded in the moment, without turning away, defending, or withdrawing. It is to meet each unfolding experience just as it is, without resistance. This leads to a calm stillness in which words arise without force.

Zen takes us to this stillness. Zen is not a label, a category, a philosophy, or a process that is applied to life. It is the breath already there, the awareness that lies beneath all of our actions. In every age, those who practiced Zen found its shape in the life they were given. A sword drawn without hatred. A brush lifted without hesitation. A bowl offered without asking. Presence is not tied to any form; it is revealed by how we meet the form that appears.

So too, conflict. Conflict is the closed door that never reopened, the friend who stopped replying, the colleague who withdrew after a harsh exchange. It may surface as an unexpected dispute, a silence between people who once shared everything, or a message that terminates an association. These are the moments this book attends to.

These stories often return to presence because it is what allows us to meet conflict without defense, without retreat, and without the need to prevail. It is not a state to be achieved, but a way of being we return to, again and again, in conversation, in quietness and in the space between. Presence invites you to notice fully. To listen with your whole being. To slow down when tensions rise. To see clearly. And to discover that conflict, met with this clear seeing, opens doors to deeper connection.

Presence is not passive. It is the most courageous act we can offer. Because it demands that we stop hiding. It asks that we stay even when we do not know the outcome. It asks that we give up the illusion of control and meet this moment without defenses.

When you are in conflict, it is tempting to search for the right move. The perfect reply. The way to repair or resolve. But what matters most is whether you are fully present for the other. Whether you are listening with the whole body. Whether you can stand motionless in the water of words without reacting to every ripple or wave. Not seeking to prevail, to dominate, or even to understand. Only to remain. And in that remaining, begin to see the other not as an opponent, not as a problem, but as a person caught in a living instant, just as you are. Voices, gestures, silences all become part of the field of being you now share.

The stories in this book do not offer solutions. They do not teach how to repair what may be broken. Instead, they offer a way to alter a viewpoint, to see what can happen when we pause, breathe, and return to what is actually here, beyond emotion, beyond defense.

This book speaks through the voice of a fictional Zen teacher. He is not a historical figure or a lineage representative. He serves as a guide who invites you to your own experience. The teacher's stories, although fictional, come from lived truth, offered by one who has learned that listening often teaches more than speaking. Each narrative offers an experience between this teacher and you. He invites you to view conflict not as an enemy to be conquered, but as a field in which to cultivate clear seeing, free of familiar distortions.

The stories may be read in any order. Like stones placed across water, there is space between them for your own step. Take what interests you, what resonates with your own journey. Leave the rest. And when the next heated moment comes, as it surely will, return. Return to the breath. Return to what is here, before explanation. This returning is not a onetime act, but a life's work. Presence is built, breath-to-breath, through a thousand choices. Do not aim to master these conversations. Aim to stay awake within them. This is not a method. It is a Way. Let us walk it together.

PART I

Discovering Presence

Building Confidence with Everyday Conflicts

Prologue

The Cup Was Full

I was in a café near the edge of a port city. The walls were cracked with salt air and time, and the windows looked out toward the harbor. The chairs were mismatched. The tea was hot, but not good. Still, I lingered.

At the table beside mine, a man and a woman sat with two cups between them. One spoke quickly. The other not at all. I could not hear the words, nor did I try to. What reached me was not content, but body language. The man leaned forward, as if chasing the sound of his own voice. The woman leaned slightly back, not retreating, but bracing.

Then, without hesitation, she took her cup and drank all of it in one motion. She set it down, stood, and left.

He remained. His hands moved toward the empty cup but did not touch it. The space between them did not change. It simply ceased to include her.

It was a fleeting instant. A cup emptied. A pause unshared.

And yet I watched him sit there for a long time.

Later, as I walked through the old quarter of the city, I passed the market. Vendors were folding tarps, sweeping their stalls. A child ran through the alley dragging a paper ribbon. The wind caught it. The ribbon twisted behind her like a loose thought.

I sat on a low wall and thought of the cup again. The way it was emptied without hesitation. Not dramatically. Not carelessly. But completely. There was no gesture toward later. No saving of the last sip. No postponement. Just now. And then done.

That, too, is presence.

Often, we think of presence as quiet. A person seated in silent tranquillity. A mind empty of thought. But there is also presence in action. In the fullness of a single movement that leaves nothing behind.

We spend much of our lives holding back. Waiting for the perfect time. Reserving judgment. Saving our clarity for when it will be better received. Holding our truth until we believe the other can understand it. We portion out ourselves in measured doses, as if our aliveness were a quantity to be budgeted.

But presence is not what we ration. It is what we release.

To be here, fully, now, is not to abandon thought. It is to let go of what is not needed in this breath. Not because it is wrong, but because it is not now.

Regret is not now.

Hope is not now.

Even understanding is not now.

Now is the cup lifted, the tea swallowed, the pause between sound and sound.

In conflict, we often try to prepare ourselves by stepping ahead. We rehearse, defend, imagine what the other will say. We draft responses to words not yet spoken. The moment comes, and we are not there. We have left our place at the table to argue with the future.

The woman who drank her tea and left may not have done so out of realization. I do not know her story. But her gesture struck a familiar resonance in me. That quality of completeness. That refusal to fragment. That commitment to whatever now is.

It reminded me of the way a bell rings when struck with the right measure. Not more, not less. Just the sound of this instant.

Presence asks nothing from what was before. It requires no promise from what comes next. It is the courage to stay here, even when the mind insists on leaving. Even when the heart aches for resolution or explanation.

To be present is to empty the cup without needing to refill it. To speak the word that is true now, without waiting for the right reply. To listen without waiting to be heard.

When time unfolds its hand, when the other looks at you, or looks away, do not wait for the perfect version of yourself to appear. Do not delay your presence until the conditions feel safe or complete.

Sit where you are.

Speak only what is needed.

Drink the tea.

And when the cup is empty, set it down.

Then walk.

Then breathe.

Then begin again.

2

The Table and the Debt

Meeting Force with Stillness

There was the melodic ring of the bell as I stepped inside. The air was redolent with the smells of cooked fish and soy sauce. My nephew's restaurant was a narrow place, the kind where the laminate tables appear too small for the plates. An overhead fan, superfluous to the air conditioning, turned silently. The walls, made of lightly finished wood slats, were decorated with black and white photographs of neighborhood street scenes. There was the distinctive sound of plates clattering in the kitchen.

My nephew, seated at a rear table, motioned for me to join him. He had asked for my advice. His face was drawn, the lines at his mouth deeper than I remembered. He spoke in a low voice, as if the walls could overhear.

"The *shobadai* is due," he said. As he spoke he folded and unfolded the edges of a napkin. "I have no money left. After the pandemic... the customers never returned in the same numbers. Many of our regulars have disappeared. He shook his head, "I can't cover all of the invoices." The late afternoon light turned the walls a warm gold.

The bell over the door rang as two men entered.

They wore dark suits, almost identical, the fabric creased in the same way. Their crewcuts were close, severe, their faces angular and hard at the edges. The older man led, his hands loose at his sides, the younger trailing half a step behind. The air seemed to tighten as they moved through the room.

The older man's eyes swept the space once, resting briefly on me, then locking onto my nephew.

He spoke softly. "Nakamura-san."

My nephew froze, the napkin falling from his hands onto the floor.

"We had an agreement," the man said.

My nephew's voice came out small.

"I know. I... things have been difficult."

The man raised a hand, palm outward. His fingers were long, the nails trimmed clean.

"Please," he said. "No stories. We all have our troubles."

He glanced at me again, his eyes narrowing slightly.

"And you are?"

"I'm his uncle," I said.

"A monk," he said, as if noting the weather.

I inclined my head, nothing more.

The younger man's knee bumped the table. The soy sauce bottle rattled against a bottle of tabasco.

The older man's attention returned to my nephew.

"The *shobadai* is two months late," he said.

My nephew's hands twisted in his lap. "I don't have enough," he whispered.

The man leaned forward, his fingers tapping on the tabletop.

"You know what to expect when obligations are ignored."

His calm voice was almost warm. The younger man's gaze narrowed as he looked menacingly at my nephew, his fingers tapping once on the table, a small, click of sound.

I watched them, my arms and hands off the table.

"You've been here many times before," I said gently, looking at the older man.

He glanced at me, a flicker of curiosity crossing his face.

He tilted his head slightly, "Enough times."

"And each time," I replied, "you found him here."

The older man's mouth twitched, barely a movement.

"Until the day we don't," he said.

I nodded.

"Until the day you don't."

A small boy outside shouted to a friend, his voice carrying down the street.

I looked at the older man.

"You must carry many stories," I said.

His eyes widened slightly. "Stories?"

"From the places you visit. The *shakkin*, the debts. The *yakusoku yaburi*, the broken promises.

He studied me with a fixed gaze.

"You think this is about stories?" he asked.

I let the question rest. The younger man's eyes darted from me to my nephew, a faint sneer tugging at his mouth.

"You think we're here for talk?"

I looked at him gently.

"You are here for the *shobadai*," I said. "But you are also here because you care about the street. About the shop. About what happens to it."

The younger man scoffed, but the older man's gaze did not change.

"Care." he repeated the word as though it were from an obscure foreign language.

"Yes," I said. "Care is different in every face. But it is there."

The fan creaked overhead. A faint smell of miso drifted from the kitchen.

The older man sat back.

"You are a strange monk," he said. "You sit here so calm. Do you think calm is stronger than power?"

"Calm is not stronger. Not weaker. It is what does not push or pull."

"Then it is weak."

"Perhaps so," I said. "However, weakness does not break. It bends like bamboo and returns. I see a man who comes himself. Not sending others. Who sits at the table. Who asks for what is due, face-to-face."

He tilted his head.

"And what do you see in him?" he gestured toward my nephew, who glanced up then, his eyes looking at me directly for the first time.

"I see a man who does not run," I said.

"I... I didn't want to hide," my nephew's voice was barely more than a whisper. "I only wanted to keep this place. My father built it. I thought if I could just..." His voice trailed off.

The older man watched him with interest.

I spoke quietly, "sometimes, the most difficult thing is to stay."

"Your nephew owes money. Not prayers. Not philosophy."

"Yes. But you collect not only money. You collect the history of this place, the hours worked, the meals cooked. The *shobadai* is not only yen."

"Then tell me, monk, what else is owed?"

"Respect for what has been built. Care for what protects the street. The payment is not denominated in only what you take, but also in what you leave behind."

The older man was silent for several seconds. "Your way of speaking is not like the others."

"Each of us carries a different weight. I carry what I have seen: men who demand, and men who give. I have seen both crumble when the storm comes."

"And what do you see in me?"

"A man who is tired. And a man who has a choice."

He exhaled through his nose, a low sound, almost like a sigh. "You're right about one thing," he said. "I came because it's my job. And because it's my street."

There was a fire burning beneath the surface of his gaze.

"And you, monk. You sit here like nothing touches you."

"It touches me," I said. "But it does not own me."

The silence stretched between us. The younger man moved slightly, waiting, but the older man did not speak.

The light outside had dimmed further with the arrival of dusk. A truck rumbled past, its engine low and even.

The older man's fingers drummed on the table, then stopped. He exhaled slowly and pushed his chair back, the legs scraping lightly against the floor.

"Not today," he said in a low voice.

He stood and adjusted the sleeves of his suit jacket. For a second, his eyes met mine, then slid to my nephew. "Take care of this place. Don't let it fall apart."

They turned, the bell above the door rang as they left.

My nephew sat quietly, the tension in his shoulders had eased.

"Thank you," he whispered, not looking at me.

I slid the plate of pickled radish closer to him.

"Eat," I said quietly.

We sat together in the quiet. The world outside moved on.

3

The Question
Remaining Present in a Public Challenge

I was asked to speak at a small university in the suburbs of the city. I have spoken often in such places. The room was plain: white walls, metal chairs, the buzz of fluorescent lights. The topic, they had told me, was "Stillness in Times of Discord."

I stood beside the podium, rather than behind it and looked out at rows of students. My talk was slow and informal, as though I were chatting with a friend. I spoke of listening. Of breathing before speaking. Of the space that opens when we do not rush to defend our position. I said that in each of us, there is a still point that does not vanish even in the worst conflicts.

When I finished, the room was silent for a breath or two. Then came the first question. A woman asked about communication with her parents. A man asked how to respond to anger in the workplace. I answered as best I could. Slowly. Briefly. Without ornament.

Then a young man stood. His voice was harsh and cold.

"Don't you think all of this is a way of avoiding reality?"

I looked at him. "What do you mean?" I asked.

"This whole thing. All this talk about presence and listening and breathing. You say it helps people deal with conflict, but what it really does is help them feel better while doing nothing. You say don't defend yourself, don't try to win. Isn't that just a way of giving up?"

The room had grown quiet. Several students glanced at one another. Someone coughed.

"Go on," I said.

He stepped forward. "I used to believe in this stuff. I thought if I studied hard, stayed focused, I could make a difference. Make our world better."

He paused, perhaps searching for the right words.

"And then last year," he continued, "my sister was harassed by one of her professors. She reported it. Nothing happened. He continues to work here. You know what I did? I went to the dean. I protested. I wrote letters. And when I told my meditation group, they said: 'Breathe through your anger. Don't react. Be present.'"

He looked directly at me.

"Presence didn't help her. And it didn't help me."

"You're saying," I began, "that quiet felt like silence. That presence felt like permission. That you needed action, not equanimity."

He gave a slight nod.

"And when you searched for inner stability, the teachings that once guided you felt distant and silent."

"Yes," he said in a subdued voice.

I waited for the echo of his response to settle. I did not hurry them away.

"You said you worked hard to make a change. And when nothing changed, presence felt like surrender."

He said nothing.

"But what if perseverance doesn't mean submission? What if it means staying with what's hard, even when you feel betrayed by it? What if it means standing in front of someone who misuses their power, not with rage that burns you from within, but with clarity that doesn't flinch?"

"That sounds nice," he said. "But clarity doesn't remove people from positions of power."

"No," I said. "But it allows you to act without becoming what you oppose."

He looked away, then back.

"You said people told you not to react. I would have told you: Let your anger come. Let it burn cleanly. But don't let it drive. Let it speak. But don't let it speak for you."

He looked up.

"Zen isn't against action," I said. "It asks only that when you act, you do not act from fear, from pride, from vengeance."

"Then how do I act?"

"You act from the part of you that watched your sister suffer and didn't look away. The part that brought this story here. The part that stood up not just for her, but for everyone else who needed someone to say what you just said."

The room was quiet Not tense, only alert.

He looked down, hands clasped tightly.

"You don't need to solve everything today," I said. "And you don't need to stop being angry. But you do need to know what matters enough to return to."

He looked at me.

"It may not get easier," I said. "But you will get clearer."

He said nothing.

"Thank you," he said and bowed. Not deeply. Not formally. Just enough. And returned to his seat.

The next student raised her hand, voice low and gentle.

Presence is not the absence of anger. It is the refusal to be led by it. It is not passivity. And it is not retreat.

To be present in conflict is to remain rooted when the heat rises, to stay open when the impulse is to shut down, to meet another's force without collapsing or hardening in return.

Presence is not a resolution to a conflict. It is the ground from which a different kind of strength can grow.

4

Sharp Words

Meeting Anger with Presence

It happened on the street outside a train station. Not in a temple court-yard. Not in a meeting hall. Just an ordinary sidewalk, near the place where the taxi queue bends.

I had just arrived from a nearby town. I was in plain robes, traveling light. A woman passed me, paused, then turned back.

"You," she said. "Do you remember me?"

Her voice had a sharpness that pulled me fully into the moment.

I looked at her face. Her name returned slowly. I had not seen her in more than a decade. Years ago, she had attended a weekend retreat I had led. A short program on breath and stillness, held at a public hall by the sea.

"Yes," I said. "We met some time ago."

She stepped closer. "You gave a talk. You said words matter. That what we say leaves a mark."

I nodded.

She pointed at me. "Then why did you not answer my question?"

I said nothing. The sidewalk around us continued as before. Wheels rolled. Shoes moved. Announcements echoed. But we were in a still pocket, just the two of us.

She continued. "I asked you something real. I wrote you after that retreat. A long letter. I told you what I was going through. You didn't write back. Nothing. No answer."

I remembered the letter. I had read it. It was long, full of hurt. She had spoken about her father, about betrayal, about words spoken too harshly to take back. I remembered sitting with it, unsure how to respond. I had placed it on my altar for a week, then another. I had bowed to it daily. And then, I had said nothing.

Now she was standing in front of me, her face tight, her voice shaking.

"You taught about presence," she said. "You spoke about being with what is difficult. But when I reached out, you disappeared."

There was a pause then.

I let my breath settle to step out of my defense. The impulse to explain was there. To say I had read the letter. To say I had cared. To say I had wanted to reply and hadn't known how.

But I said none of those things.

Instead, I bowed.

"I left you alone in pain," I said. "And that was not kind."

The edge in her eyes did not soften, but she did not move away.

"You could have said anything," she said. "Even just one line."

I nodded. "Yes."

"I needed to be seen."

I said, "And now, I do see you."

She stood still. The silence that followed was not absence. It had weight.

We remained like that for several breaths. Then someone brushed past us on the sidewalk. A boy dropped a coin. A car horn sounded somewhere nearby.

She stepped back slightly. Her shoulders dropped. She looked down, then away.

"I'm tired of carrying this," she said.

"You do not have to carry it alone."

She looked at me again. Not with ease. Not with forgiveness. But with something less guarded.

"You could have said that before," she said.

"I am saying it now."

She looked down once more, then nodded once. Not agreement, but acknowledgment. Then she turned and walked into the station.

Sometimes, we meet anger directly. Not hidden. Not polite. Just raw, rising energy aimed in our direction.

The usual reflex is one of three: defend, retreat, or counterattack. These are the stances we are taught in early life. Protect the self. Withdraw from danger. Argue the point.

But there is another way.

When anger comes, it does not always seek an answer. Often, it seeks recognition. To be heard. To be met without judgment or correction. When we meet anger with silence alone, it can feel like disregard. But when we meet it with presence, followed by one true sentence, we create the space for connection to return.

There is a kind of stillness that is avoidance. And there is a kind of stillness that listens.

To pause is not to disappear. It is to remain without closing.

When I stood on that sidewalk, I did not reach for resolution. I reached for ground. The place where her pain could be real, and my attention could be steady.

That was enough.

I thought of her words: "I needed to be seen."

That is the true heat beneath most conflict. Not the disagreement. Not the insult. But the pain of invisibility. When someone speaks in anger, they are often asking, without knowing how, "Do you see me now?"

If we can say yes, not with agreement, not with apology we do not mean, but with presence, then something shifts.

Even if nothing is resolved. Even if no forgiveness comes. Something shifts.

When anger comes to your door, do not greet it with armor. Do not greet it with silence that hides. Do not greet it with cleverness or retreat.

Stand still. Breathe.

Let your body say, "I am here."

Let your eyes say, "I am listening."

And when the moment comes, say just one true thing. Not to end the conflict, but to show that the other person is not alone.

Words spoken from presence are few. But they are remembered. Even if the wound is deep. Even if you cannot undo what was done. The bridge begins in the pause. And in the sentence that follows.

5

The Fox Beneath the Cedar

Compassion Without Clinging

I was clearing snow from the pathway behind the tool shed. Under the low branches of a cedar, I saw some red fur beneath the brush. It appeared at first as a drift of leaves and pine needles. However, when I stepped closer, I saw that it was a small fox with one hind leg stretched at an unnatural angle. When I knelt beside her she turned her head and looked at me.

Tucked in my sleeve was a cloth, a scrap that was once used for wrapping garden tools. I unfolded it and laid it beside her. She remained quietly motionless.

I returned to the shed, found a shallow bowl, and filled it with water from the flask I carried. When I came back, she hadn't moved. I placed the bowl near the cloth and stepped back.

Through the morning, I stayed close, working slowly. Where her body rested, the snow gave way to bare ground, a dark oval of exposed earth.

That evening, I told no one.

The next morning, she was there. She had not touched the water. Her breathing was thinner now, like the sound of pine needles brushing the wind. I changed the cloth and brought another bowl, this time with a few soaked grains of rice. She did not move.

A novice noticed me returning to the slope and followed. He was young, eager to help, his eyes always searching for instruction.

"Are you caring for an animal, Master?" he asked.

I said nothing, only handed him the empty bowl.

He returned with me the next day, and the next. Each time we came, we brought no intention to heal or fix. Only presence. The fox blinked slowly when we arrived. Once, she lifted her head slightly and lowered it again. That was all.

On the fourth day, she was gone.

There was no sign of struggle, no blood, no tracks in the snow beyond the soft impression where she had lain. It was as if the forest had reclaimed her without effort. The bowl was tipped slightly, the cloth folded by the wind.

The novice was quiet.

"Should we look for her?" he asked.

I shook my head.

"But what if she is hurt?"

I let the question hang in the air. A gust moved through the cedars. A branch released a small heap of snow onto the ground. The world continued, unchanged.

We buried the cloth beneath the cedar and placed the empty bowl upside down on a flat stone nearby. I lit a single stick of incense and stood silently as the smoke curled into the air, disappearing.

No words. No sutras. Only attention.

Later that week, during tea, the novice asked again, more carefully this time:

"Master, should we have done more?"

I looked at the steam curling from my cup. I placed it down gently.

"More of what?"

He frowned, unsure. "Help. Medicine. Shelter. We could have taken her inside."

"We could have. And perhaps she would have lived another day. Or perhaps the scent of humans would have frightened her. Maybe she would have tried to flee and worsened her injury. Perhaps she needed the cold."

He looked puzzled. "But we should have tried."

"We did try," I said. "We tried to be with her."

There is a form of compassion that seeks to erase all suffering. But there is another quieter, slower way that seeks only to be present within it. The fox did not need our pity. She needed the dignity of not being owned by her pain, or by our need to resolve it.

She was not our student. Not our pet. Not our lesson. She was herself. A creature shaped by wind and hunger, age and injury. A flicker of awareness passing through this world, as we all are.

A week passed, then two.

I found a tuft of red fur caught in a low branch. I left it there.

In spring, I returned to the cedar. The ground had settled unevenly where thaw and frost had traded places through the season. The bowl was resting upside down on the stone just as I had left it. At the stone's base, early green shoots had pushed through, the persistent growth that rises from undisturbed soil.

Not all suffering calls for rescue. Not all pain requires intervention. Sometimes our role is not to cure or correct, but to attend. To sit beside what cannot be mended and offer it nothing but our whole attention.

This is the heart of discussion. Not persuading. Not conquering. Not even agreeing. But sharing space with another being, without needing them to change for us to remain.

She came wounded. She left in silence. We did not heal her. We did not harm her. We were there.

The wind continues its path. The fox continues hers. And we continue ours.

6

The Accusation

Listening Without Defense

It was not long ago, and not far from here. A lay practitioner had come to speak with me. We had known each other for many years. He had attended countless retreats. Sat in silence with care and discipline. I had officiated at his mother's memorial and once sat with him for hours when he was too ashamed to speak.

But this day, he was not calm. He entered the small reception room with his breath already tight, words just behind it. His face was drawn. His eyes restless. A pressure had been building over time and now it had found a crack.

"You've been unfair," he said, before I could offer tea.

I said nothing.

"You are available for everyone but me. You listen to their questions, answer with stories, share tea with the ones who've been here less than a year. And I..." He stopped himself, but the heat continued to rise.

"I have served here for eight years," he said. "And I feel like a tolerated guest. You answer my questions with silence. You give me work but not trust. You look at me like I'm not quite ready. Always not quite ready."

I did not respond. I let the words pass through the room and settle where they landed.

He looked at me with expectation and also dread. He had come to speak, but also to see if I would fail him.

And perhaps, in some ways, I had.

I said, "You feel unseen."

He swallowed. "Yes."

"You've worked hard. You've practiced well. And you've felt held at a distance."

"Yes," he said again. "Exactly."

I let that be true. Not because I agreed with his every word, but because I could feel the truth behind them. He was not asking for my defense. He was asking to be heard.

"You're angry," I said.

"Yes."

"You're hurt."

His shoulders lowered. "Yes."

We sat for a while. The wind outside passed through the cracks in the door frame. A wooden floorboard creaked as the building adjusted to the day.

Finally, I said, "I didn't answer your questions because they came too quickly."

He looked up.

"You asked them from the surface of the mind. I didn't answer because I wanted to wait until *you* were asking."

His mouth opened. Then closed.

I continued, "And I waited too long."

"I don't want your approval," he said. "I just want to be real here."

"Then be real," I said.

His brow furrowed.

"Even when I seem distant, even when I don't respond how you hope, be real. Not careful. Not worthy. Just present."

He exhaled. "That's not easy."

"No," I said. "It is not."

He looked down at the floor, as if unsure where to direct his gaze.

"You don't have to prove anything," I said. "But I understand why it has felt that way."

He said nothing.

After some time, I poured tea. We drank without ceremony. Just two people in a room.

Presence in conflict is not passivity. It is a kind of smoldering fire. It does not explain itself. It does not guard the heart. But it also does not disappear.

When we are blamed, we want to justify. When we are hurt, we want to retreat. When we are misunderstood, we want to correct. But presence does not reach for protection.

It listens for the person beneath the noise. And when it speaks, it does not defend. It names what has been unseen. It joins the other in the room, even if the air has not cooled. Some conflicts cannot be solved. But they can be entered. Fully. Gently. Without fear. And from there, a new way forward can begin.

7

Two Arrows

The Second Wound

It was a cold winter evening with intermittent rain. I had just concluded a talk about presence in conflictual conversations. On my way to the exit, a woman from the audience approached. She introduced herself by saying that she was a physician at the local hospital.

"My patient died today," she said. "An eight-year old girl. I made a mistake," she hesitated and then continued. "I missed a truth I wasn't ready to see."

She looked down. "I cannot stop thinking about it. Replaying it. Questioning every decision."

I did not reply immediately, inviting silence to establish space for her grief.

"Are you familiar with Buddha's teaching about two arrows?" I asked. She shook her head.

"When a tough event occurs, we are hit by two arrows. The first arrow is the event itself, the physical pain, the loss, the unavoidable suffering that life contains. This arrow cannot always be avoided. It is part of being human."

Outside, the rain intensified. Its rhythm on the roof created a gentle percussion.

"The second arrow is our reaction to the first. It is our judgment, the story we create about our pain. 'I could have prevented this.' 'I don't deserve this.' 'This is too much to bear.' This is the arrow that we shoot into ourselves."

She was silent for a long time. "So, my patient's death is the first arrow."

"Yes."

"And my self-judgment is the second."

"Yes."

She considered this. "But doesn't the second arrow serve a purpose? Without it, how would I learn from my mistakes? How would I improve?"

"You ask an important question. The problem is not in seeing clearly what happened or taking responsibility. The problem comes when the second arrow becomes a weapon of self-punishment rather than a tool for growth."

She looked down at her hands. "It feels impossible to separate the two."

"Watch the rain," I said, gesturing toward the window. "It falls on the earth without judgment. It doesn't fall harder on the places that 'deserve' it. Then, from this falling, flowers grow."

I continued. "Can you hold your error in the same way? Not as a fault demanding punishment, but as water that, though painful, might nourish growth?"

A small change passed through her bearing. Not relaxation, exactly, but the quiet release that comes when a new way of seeing begins to emerge.

"How do I stop shooting the second arrow?" she asked.

"You begin by recognizing it," I said. "When you feel the sting of the first arrow, the honest grief of losing your patient, stay with that feeling. When you notice yourself adding judgment, 'I should have known, I should have done differently,' name it: 'This is the second arrow.'"

The rain was slowing now. Drops fell from the eaves, punctuating the space between us.

"The second arrow feels protective," she said. "As if by punishing myself, I can prevent this from happening again."

"Yes," I replied. "That's how it disguises itself. But presence doesn't need punishment to learn. It needs clear seeing and an open heart."

"It's not about avoiding the second arrow completely, is it? That's not possible."

"No," I said. "It's about recognizing when we've picked up the bow. And perhaps, with practice, setting it down a little sooner each time."

In conflict, we are often struck by two arrows. The first is the difficulty itself: a rejection, a failure, a loss. This arrow may cause genuine pain. But the second arrow, our judgment about what happened, our stories about what it means about us or others, our amplification of suffering through rumination, this is the arrow we can learn to avoid.

When someone speaks harsh words to you, that is the first arrow. When you ask yourself, "Why am I always treated this way?" or "What did I do to deserve this?" that is the second arrow. When your best attempt fails, that is the first arrow. When you berate yourself, "I will never succeed," you have been struck by the second arrow.

Presence allows us to feel the first arrow clearly, without the added suffering of the second. This doesn't mean we become passive or fail to address problems. Rather, we respond from clarity instead of reactivity. We see what is, not what our fear tells us.

In each disturbing instant ask yourself: "Am I feeling unavoidable pain from this situation, or am I shooting myself with a second arrow? Am I responding to what is happening, or to the narrative I'm creating about it?"

The ability to distinguish between the two arrows takes time to acquire. However, like all practice, it deepens over time. Each fleeting instant of awareness forms a space, a breath, in which choice becomes possible.

8

The Noble Friend
The Gift of Growth in Opposition

The Buddha spoke of the noble friend, the *kalyāṇa-mitta*. The noble friend is not a companion of convenience or comfort, but one who walks beside us with presence and integrity. A noble friend is not always agreeable. He may disturb our certainties. He may speak truths we do not wish to hear. Yet when his words are offered without malice, they become mirrors, reflecting not just who we are, but what we have yet to see.

It was many years ago, early in my time of teaching. I had been asked to lead a discussion for a group of visiting lay practitioners, doctors, teachers, parents, retirees, each bringing his own life into the hall. Among them was a man who, from the start, made his position known. He questioned nearly every point. He interrupted. He spoke with clipped certainty, eyes narrowed not in malice but in judgment. It was not anger he brought into the room, but resistance honed into challenge.

He did not believe in the validity of monastic life. He made that clear. He said it was too removed from the world's demands, too sheltered to offer anything useful to those who lived "in the real world." Each time he spoke, I could feel my jaw tighten, breath quicken. My thoughts moved quickly but not toward understanding. They rushed toward defense.

At one point, I gently corrected a misquotation. He laughed. "You monks love your riddles," he said. "But real life doesn't work that way."

As all eyes turned to me, I could feel tension in the room. Long ago, I would have responded to his remark with firmness. I would paraphrase the teachings and clarify the difference between misunderstanding and truth. However, in that juncture, an older truth surfaced. It was the teaching that everyone we meet is part of our path. And those who challenge us are perhaps most important of all.

I did not correct him again. I said, "You may be right. Life outside these walls does ask different things from life within them. Would you be willing to share what shaped your view?"

He hesitated for a breath and then spoke of his work in a hospital ER, the heavy responsibilities of choices made under pressure. He described the cost of caring too much in a system that asked for too much. And then, unexpectedly, he said, "That may be the reason I came here today. I'm tired of urgency."

That sentence hung in the air.

It was not persuasion that opened that space nor was it debate. It was presence. The willingness to meet him as he was, without defense, without recoil. To see him not as a threat, but as a noble friend.

We often believe conflict is either to be resolved or avoided. But some oppositions are not meant to be erased. They are meant to be met. A noble friend, by confronting us with our blind spots, may evoke our reactivity. He may stir our attachment to being right, or strike at those places in which identity clings. But if we can remain open, his resistance can become the doorway to clarity. His presence can become the source of insight.

This is not to glorify conflict. Some voices do wound. Some arguments are not rooted in shared truth but in harm. Boundaries are necessary. Protection is sometimes the most compassionate act. But many of the confrontations we shrink from are the friction between differing truths. Each truth is shaped by its own story. Its own sorrow. Its own longing.

It is easy to retreat into defensiveness and cloak it in the robes of conviction. But when we do, we close the gate through which understanding may enter.

Shāntideva, an Indian monk, wrote in the eighth century, "Where would I find a friend as kind as my enemy, who shows me the path to awakening?"

The one who angers us is the one who reveals what is unsettled within us. The one who disagrees may be the one who invites us to deepen our listening.

When next you find yourself in conflict, pause. Rather than reacting, ask: What is this person showing me? What is being asked of me in this occasion? What truth, hidden beneath my resistance, is waiting to be seen?

These questions do not dissolve disagreement. But they temper the field on which it plays out. They alter the terrain from combat to curiosity. From reaction to responsiveness.

The man who challenged me returned a year later. He bowed, murmuring his appreciation, before sitting. When our conversation ended, he lingered. "I've been thinking about that talk," he said. "It stayed with me."

I bowed in return. "It stayed with me too."

Not every conflict is resolved. But every encounter can become part of the path, if we are willing to meet the other not as an adversary, but as a companion showing us where our work remains.

The noble friend is not always kind in tone, but he is kind in purpose. He is the one who does not let us remain asleep. He holds the mirror even when we would rather turn away. And through him, we learn to see not just the other, but ourselves.

After the Misstep

When Guidance Wounds

I remember a young monk who stayed only a short while. He carried himself like a bird just before flight: quiet and alert. Not resistance, but a hush around him, as if he were always listening for a sound that meant correction.

One afternoon, after garden sweeping, I found him adjusting the stones around the temple path. They had been dislodged during a rainstorm. I approached and offered a suggestion about the pattern. He moved one stone, then hesitated.

I pointed again.

His hands did not move.

I misunderstood.

I thought he had not grasped what I meant, so I crouched beside him and reached for one of the stones myself.

"Like this," I said.

He froze. Then stood and bowed with a quiet word of thanks and walked away.

I remained crouched, one hand resting on the stone.

Later, at evening tea, he did not speak. When I offered him a glance, he lowered his eyes.

I said nothing that night.

The next day, he was gone.

His *shikibuton* had been folded into thirds. His robes were neatly placed beside it. No letter. No explanation.

I asked the abbot.

"He left before dawn," he said.

"Did he speak to you?"

"No."

He looked at me with calm eyes.

"You said a few words?"

"I tried to help," I said.

Sometimes harm is not what we intend. Sometimes it is what we overlook. A touch of assumption. A trace of impatience. A failure to read what the other has not said aloud.

I thought about that point in time. I had not raised my voice. I had not acted in anger. I had offered only instruction. But it may have been my tone, or the moment I chose, or how close I stood that caused the door to close before it could fully open.

It is easy to offer apologies when the damage is obvious. When the act is deliberate. The words are inappropriate. The roles are clear. But what of the harm we do in passing? The intervals when we press too soon, or too hard, or not at all, and only afterward feel the echo of absence.

I never saw him again. But I carried the shape of that day like a pebble in a shoe.

Weeks later, during evening rounds, I found myself walking on the garden path. The stones were in disarray. I knelt and began to adjust them. Slowly. Without plan. Just listening with my hands.

A novice passed, paused, and asked, "Is there a right way to place them?"

I said, "Only to notice where the footing will be as you place them."

I kept working. The pattern would never be perfect. It was not meant to be. But it could be tended.

Presence after harm is not performance. It is not speaking quickly to smooth the air. It is not returning to the other with prepared phrases and hopeful tones. Sometimes the other is gone. Sometimes he will not speak again. Sometimes the only thing left is the discomfort. And that must be met, too. With undisturbed calm. With the willingness to feel the edge of what was broken and not look away.

There is a kind of silence that opens after harm. The silence of what was overlooked. What was not held with enough care.

If you have caused harm, even unknowingly, let the discomfort be your teacher. Let it slow your movements. Let it deepen your gaze. Let it remind you of what is unseen in others.

Feel what you missed. Feel what the other may have felt. And let that change how you place your words.

No apology, however skillful, can undo a closing. But presence may help you walk with greater care the next time the path is uneven.

Not all harm can be repaired. But all harm can be met.

10

The Returned Statue
What Remains

I remember a contentious meeting in Tokyo which took place in a conference room in the U.S. Cultural Affairs Office. The walls were adorned with framed pictures: Mount Fuji, cherry trees in blossom in Washington, several Hiroshige and Utamaro woodblock prints. On the table were folders and porcelain cups of coffee. We were meeting to discuss the future of an object that was not present, a small bodhisattva statue in gilt-bronze, more than a thousand years old. It remained in Washington, in a museum archive, awaiting the outcome of our discussion.

Five people, including myself, were seated at the table. There was an American diplomat from the Cultural Antiquities Task Force. He had a neat stack of documents in front of him and a calm voice. From South Korea came two officials: one from the national museum, the other a historian known for his work on Japanese colonial appropriation. Their tone, even before speaking, was tense. Finally, there was the Special Envoy for Cultural Heritage from the Japanese Ministry of Foreign Affairs.

I had been sent by the abbot to be the voice of our monastery. The abbot had been clear. "You are to speak for what cannot speak," he said. The Americans agreed to my role after the temple provided documentation proving the statue had once stood in our side altar. The Koreans objected, stating that I could not be neutral. But they conceded when the U.S. host explained that I was not a representative of the Japanese government. I was present only for the temple itself. Even so, I could feel that the Korean representatives saw me as a stand-in for the nation they had not forgiven.

The American opened the meeting with a summary of the issue. The statue had resurfaced after seventy years, found in the estate of a U.S. military officer stationed in Japan during the Occupation. The temple in question, he noted, claimed it had been taken without consent.

The Korean representative, a professor from Seoul University, gestured toward the folder in front of him. "The casting technique reflects the advanced skills developed in Korea during the late Baekje period. The statue's hand position, facial structure, style of crown, and drapery folds are all distinctive characteristics of Baekje Buddhist sculpture. This proves its identification as a work of Korean origin."

The Japanese representative, his hands folded on the table, replied without lifting his eyes. "We do not agree. In those early centuries Korean artisans were invited to Japan. Some Japanese bodhisattva statues were made by these craftsmen. Korean hands may be so. However, fashioned here in Japan. We have documents that prove provenance."

The professor replied, his voice controlled, while hot undertones simmered below the surface, "You speak of documents. Where were these documents when our temples were looted? When our language was banned? When Buddhist monks were forced to bow to portraits of your emperor?" He pointed aggressively to the Japanese delegate, who remained composed. "You pillage and ransack Buddhist temples. You wait for rare artifacts to be lost. Then you claim they were always yours."

The Japanese official's expression hardened. "We concede we made mistakes. But not every possession is theft. To claim otherwise is to rewrite history. There were exchanges. Gifts. Shared cultural currents long before the twentieth century."

"Exchanges?" the Korean professor snapped. "What exchange is made at gunpoint? What gift is given when names are erased?"

The younger Korean delegate leaned forward. "This statue is not an ornament. It is part of the cultural heritage of our people. It symbolizes the forced silence of the millions who were not allowed to speak. To give this sacred *bosalsang* to Japan is an insult to every Korean monk who was muzzled during decades of occupation."

The Japanese official raised his voice for the first time. "And what of the decades since? What of the treaties signed, the apologies offered? At what point is reconciliation allowed to begin?"

"Begin?" the Korean replied, now visibly angry. "You speak as if reconciliation is yours to grant. You want peace on your terms. A peace without memory."

The room had capsized into deep argument. The American diplomat tried to intercede, but his voice was ignored. Folders were flipped open; pages fluttered like agitated wings. The smell of the untouched cups of coffee had gone bitter in the air. The room filled with raised voices and the heaviness of memory, resentment, and distrust. It was not only the statue's history that was on trial. It was all of ours.

Then they turned to me. The American looked across the table. "Reverend," he said, "would you like to speak on behalf of the temple?"

I did not move. I sat with both hands resting on the table, palms down, my spine straight but unforced. I let the noise of the room settle. Not by asking for silence, but by not adding to it. There was no mask on my face, no performance in my manner. I was not waiting to speak. I was fully present with whatever arose.

The atmosphere changed. The shuffling of papers stopped. The Korean delegate leaned back, his hand holding a document he no longer waved. The Japanese official's breathing slowed. Their eyes returned to me because there was nowhere else for them to land. Without raising my voice or interrupting theirs, I remained quiet and unmoving. And silent immobility, when it does not flinch, alters everything around it. The temperature of the room changed. The fight remained, but it lost some of its edge.

I first looked at the Korean delegates. "You have carried loss," I said. "I cannot begin to understand its cost. I was born during the Greater East Asia War and raised by my grandparents. My grandfather was a simple fisherman. My grandmother never forgave the fires in Tokyo that took her sister."

Then I turned toward the Japanese official. "And you, too, carry a history. Not only what was done to us. But of what we did to others. Some carry it with denial. Some with shame. I carry it with silence."

No one responded. But their anger had thinned. Not vanished, just no longer steering the room.

"The statue cannot return itself," I continued. "It cannot speak for its origin. But it remembers where it has been. It remembers incense. It remembers sunlight through the wooden slats of the old temple hall. It remembers the hands that brushed dust from its base before morning meditation."

I let the silence return. This time it was a different kind of silence. Not void, not holding its breath. Just space. Enough for a new response to emerge.

"My temple does not claim ownership. It asks only this: that we stop holding the statue as if it were evidence. It is not a weapon used in a crime. It is not a prize. It is a reminder."

I paused, then said, "If there is uncertainty, perhaps it does not belong only in one place. Let it spend three years at our temple. Then three years in a Korean temple of your choosing. Let it keep moving between our countries to remind us that reverence is not possession."

I let the idea settle before continuing.

"Let this statue be a thread between us. A thread not pulled tight but held gently. The role of a Bodhisattva is to ease suffering. Let this one do its part. It cannot settle history, but it can offer tranquility to those who carry pain. Let it pass quietly between us, like a breath remembered."

No one argued.

Nothing was settled that day. But the ground between us no longer felt the same. The American no longer looked for loopholes. The Korean historian no longer leaned forward. The Japanese official folded his papers more slowly. No one stood up first. The argument had not ended, but its edge had tempered. No one had won. But the need to win had dissolved.

More than a year later, word came. The statue would return under shared custodianship, rotating every five years between our temple and a Korean monastery. A plaque would accompany it, bearing the following inscription in Japanese, Korean, and English: *This statue has passed through hands of reverence and hands of loss. It returns not to ownership, but to stillness.*

The message was mine. I wrote it in the hall where the statue had once stood. I did not write to explain, only to mark the turning.

The day the crate arrived, I opened it alone. I did not lift the statue. I only bowed to it with my head low and my breath deep.

When the past fills the room, let your voice be one that does not argue for the past. Let it speak for what longs to be held without fear. Presence does not win. But it remains. And in remaining, it changes what it touches. You cannot erase what was done. But you can bow to what remains.

PART II

Deepening Practice

Staying Present Through Increasing Complexity

The Time Of The Bamboo

Finding Presence in the Midst of Conflict

I was walking alone through the university botanical garden in Sapporo. The rain had passed not long before, leaving behind its trace in the moist, darkened soil and the shallow puddles that mirrored the sky. The garden was hushed. Birdsong echoed faintly from the spruce and fir trees, and the wind moved in long, even breaths.

I had no plan. Only an intent to rest somewhere undemanding. Somewhere I did not need to answer questions.

A curved stone path wound through wild grasses and low brush toward the far edge of the garden. There, I came upon a thicket of dwarf bamboo. In the dim light, it rose like a living wall, dark green and gently rustling. A wooden bench sat at the edge.

I sat down. Some time passed. Then, the sound of approaching footsteps. A woman came along the path. Her pace was quick at first but slowed as she saw me. She looked at the bamboo, then at the bench. Her face was drawn. There was a tightness around her eyes, a brittleness, an emotion left unresolved.

She sat at the far end of the bench, not quite joining me, but not hiding either. We were silent for a while.

Her breath was shallow. The breath of someone holding back more than she could say.

"You don't mind?"

I shook my head.

"Good," she said. "I want to be in a place where no one will ask me anything."

I said nothing.

After a pause, she added, "I'm supposed to be at a mediation session with my brother. It's about our father's estate."

She gave a dry laugh, brittle at the edges. "I walked out."

Her hand tightened on the bench's armrest. She released it, then gripped it again.

"I kept telling myself I had to stay in the room. Be mature. Be present. But how do you stay present when someone's calmly rewriting your life?"

The wind stirred again. The bamboo swayed.

"He claimed Dad promised him the house," she said. "A private conversation I wasn't part of. And now that Dad's gone, there's no way to verify anything."

She paused, her voice lower now.

"The worst part is how reasonable he makes it sound. As though he's just honoring Dad's wishes. The dutiful son, fulfilling an obligation."

I studied her face in profile, the tension in her jaw, the curve of her shoulders folding in on themselves, as if shielding a tenderness already bruised.

"For three years I cared for Dad," she said. "Doctor visits, medications, cleaning up after him. I quit my job. My brother didn't. But now he says Dad understood his 'financial pressures.' So, he gets the house."

Her voice dropped again. "I don't even want the house. It's not about that. It's that he's erased me from the story."

A crow called from somewhere deep in the trees. She exhaled slowly, her shoulders lowering just slightly.

"I've been trying to practice presence she said. "My therapist suggested it. You know, for family stress. Watch your thoughts. Notice your emotions. Don't react."

She shook her head.

"But all I felt in that room was rage rising like floodwater. And this process of awareness just made it worse. It made me more aware of how much I wanted to scream."

I turned toward the bamboo, then looked back at her.

"Perhaps it isn't about stepping back from your anger?" I said.

She turned to me. "What do you mean?"

"Sometimes presence may feel like standing outside yourself. Presence means staying close. Not separating from the anger. Being here with it."

She frowned. "That sounds like losing control."

"When you were trying to observe your anger in that room, did you feel more or less in control?"

She was silent a long time.

"Less," she said at last. "Much less. Like I was fighting two battles: my brother in front of me, and my own reaction inside."

The bamboo stirred again. This time, we both watched. The way each stalk bent and returned. The way the whole grove moved together while each stem kept its own rhythm.

"The bamboo doesn't fight the wind," I said. "But it doesn't observe it from a distance either. It moves with it completely."

She gave a short laugh. "But I'm not bamboo."

"No," I said. "But you're not separate from the present instant either. Your anger, your brother's denial, the room, your choice to leave, it's all part of what is actually happening."

We sat in silence.

"What was I supposed to do?" she asked. "Just let him lie about what our father wanted?"

"I don't know what you were supposed to do," I said. "But you did what you needed to do. You left when staying no longer felt possible."

"My lawyer says leaving weakened my position."

"And what does your heart say?"

She looked at the oak and maple trees, their leaves rustling in the wind.

"My heart says I couldn't breathe in there. That part of me would have withered if I had stayed and pretended it was okay."

"Then you honored what mattered more than strategy."

The wind picked up slightly. The bamboo whispered.

"I keep thinking I should have handled it better," she said. "Should have been more present, more centered. Should have found a way to respond without reacting."

"What if walking out was your response?" I said. "What if that was the most present thing you could do?"

She looked at me, surprised. "But I felt so scattered. So angry."

"Scattered according to whom? Your anger was clear. It saw what was happening and said no. That sounds present to me."

She breathed out. "I never thought of it that way."

"Presence contains stillness and storms" I said. "Sometimes it's fierce. Sometimes it says no with your whole body."

The light was fading, clouds drifting in. The bamboo glowed silvery in the afternoon dimness.

"My therapist says to stay with difficult emotions," she said. "But it always sounds like sitting passively while being stabbed."

"Perhaps staying with emotion doesn't mean being passive," I said. "Maybe it means moving like this bamboo. Flexible. Grounded. Responsive."

She watched the grove. "When I walked out," she said slowly, "it wasn't because I couldn't manage the conflict. It was because I could manage the truth. The truth that staying would have meant betraying a part of myself."

"Yes," I said. "That's presence. Not the kind that endures everything, but the kind that knows what cannot be endured."

She stood then, slower than before. No rush.

"I don't know what happens next," she said. "My brother probably thinks he's won."

"And?"

"And maybe that's fine. Maybe some battles are won by not fighting them."

She turned toward the path. "Thank you," she said. "For not fixing anything."

After she left, I remained on the bench. The bamboo swayed in the wind, each stalk finding its place, bending without resistance, never breaking.

Presence is not a method. It is not a script or a calm pose. It is the living thread that runs through each fleeting instant when we stop resisting. When we trust what we know without needing confirmation.

Sometimes it says 'yes.' Sometimes it says 'no.' Sometimes it stands still. Sometimes it walks away.

But it is always here. Like the wind through bamboo.

12

The Ladle

Not Every Fire Needs Water

It happened during morning preparation when the steam rises early and tempers rise with it. In the monastery kitchen, the largest pot is reserved for *miso shiru*, the broth we serve with nearly every meal. That morning, a new monk, only a year into training, was stirring the pot under the direction of Jun, one of our senior monks. Jun had worked in that kitchen for decades. He spoke little but expected precision.

The broth was nearly finished when I entered the kitchen. I had come to return a basket.

Jun stood watching the younger monk stir. His arms crossed. His jaw set.

"You were told not to let it boil," Jun said.

The younger monk didn't look up. "It isn't boiling."

Jun stepped forward. "You've already added the miso. Even small bubbles now are too much."

The younger monk's grip tightened around the ladle.

"I was watching it," he said. "It's not ruined."

"That's not the point."

There was the low hiss of steam as the two men faced the pot. There was a palpable tension between them.

"You said to watch it carefully," the young monk said. "I did. You speak as though I walked away."

Jun didn't raise his voice. "You were told to remove the ladle when it reaches this point. It remains in your hand."

The younger monk placed the ladle on the counter with more force than was necessary. It made a jarring sound against the wood.

"Then do it yourself," he said, and turned toward the door.

I stepped aside so he could pass. He paused when he saw me, then said, "Excuse me," bowed stiffly and left the kitchen.

Jun said nothing.

I walked to the counter, picked up the ladle, and rinsed it under the tap. The water was cold.

Jun stood where he was, facing the pot. I did not ask him to explain himself. I did not speak on behalf of the younger monk. I placed the ladle on the hook above the sink.

"I've boiled the broth myself many times," I said. "Each time, I tell myself I'll watch it better."

Jun said nothing for a while. Then: "He thinks I don't respect him."

"Do you?"

"He's learning quickly. But not everything is about skill."

"No," I said. "Not everything."

We let the silence return. The pot settled. Jun removed it from the flame and placed the lid on top.

Later that day, the younger monk returned to the kitchen without being asked. He offered no apology. Jun gave no lecture. They stood side by side at the sink, washing the morning dishes.

Their movements were focused and coordinated. Nothing more was said about the broth. Or the ladle.

Yet the atmosphere had changed.

Not because of confrontation. Not because one of them gave in. But because neither one left the room inside himself.

Presence does not mean approval. And silence does not mean agreement. But sometimes, the space between reaction and response is where clarity first appears.

And not every fire needs water. Some need us to stay near until the heat becomes light.

13

Listening for the Grain

On Patience and Opening What Is Closed

When I was a young monk, I was sometimes assigned the task of *maki-wari*, splitting wood. In those days, before we had gas or electric systems, firewood was used for heating the bathwater. The larger logs were too thick to burn well, so they were broken into smaller splits.

It was a simple task, but one that humbled me.

I would approach the woodpile with determination, choose a log, place it on the center of the chopping block and position the wedge. The wedge was iron, worn smooth by years of use. I would strike it with a wooden mallet, lifting it high and bringing it down with force.

But the log would not yield.

I struck again and again. My arms grew heavy. Sweat gathered on my brow. Nonetheless, the log resisted all of my efforts. My hands ached from the blows. My breath burned. My frustration grew.

The wedge was too old and dull. Or the log too dense. I blamed the tools, the task, the wood itself and sometimes even the weather.

One morning, as I struggled with an unyielding piece, my teacher approached. Standing beside me, he asked, "Why do you fight the wood?"

"Because it resists me," I said. "No matter how hard I strike, it will not split."

He observed for a while and then asked me to hand him the mallet. He selected a log from the wood pile and examined it carefully. He slowly ran his fingers over the rough bark and said, "Can you see this this?" He pointed to a faint line in the grain.

I saw nothing.

"It is just a log," I said.

He shook his head. "Every tree grows with a pattern, a grain. If you strike without seeing it, you go against the nature of the wood. The wedge should be positioned on this line to take advantage of the natural structure of the wood. For straight-grained wood, such as this cypress, your split will be clean and even. If you respect the wood it will not resist.

He placed the wedge along that faint line then he struck it. Not hard, not fast, but measured. On the third blow, the log split cleanly in two.

I stared. There had been no battle. No frustration. Only attention. Rhythm. Patience.

"You see?" he said. "I did not force the wood. I followed it."

I frowned. "But I used more strength. Why didn't it work for me?"

"Because you struck with effort, not with understanding. You pushed. I listened. The wood didn't open to my power. It opened to being seen."

I stood silently, the mallet warm in my hands.

"But I don't know how to see the grain," I said.

"Not yet. But you will. Stop looking for resistance. Look for where it wants to open. Feel for shadows. The grain will show you if you stop trying to break the wood and rather ask how it might come apart."

He looked at me with kindness. "This is not only true of wood."

And I understood.

I thought of conversations that had gone badly. Moments when I had pressed too hard, argued past the heart of the present, tried to convince rather than listen. I remembered the silence that followed, the way a door seemed to close in the other person's eyes. And I saw that I had been swinging without seeing. Pushing rather than pausing.

He motioned to the stump. "Try again."

I placed a new log on the block. This time, I turned it slowly. I felt its heft, ran my fingers along the bark. At first, I saw only hardness. But then, there it was. A faint subtle line, a curve in the grain.

I carefully positioned the wedge, lifted the mallet and struck, not with force, but with care. The wedge moved. I struck again. On the third blow, the log opened with a loud crack.

I stepped back, surprised by the ease of it.

My teacher smiled. "So it is with people, and with life. Strike at the right place, at the right time and the world opens to you."

Since then, I have split many logs. And spoken many words. And I have learned that it is not strength that opens what is closed but presence. Attention. Listening.

When I pause to feel for the grain in another, when I wait to see where they are ready to open, there is no need to press hard. Only to strike true.

14

Uneven Steps

Finding Rhythm in Uncertainty

One morning in early spring, I watched a man climb the temple steps alone. He had arrived while the grounds were silent before the afternoon bell. I did not recognize him. He moved like a branch bent under snow, quiet beneath a weight the world could not see. His movements were careful, not only from age or caution, but from the kind of inner strain that settles in the body when decisions do not come easily.

The stone staircase leading up to our temple gate is old. The steps ask for attention. They are of different heights by design. Some rise just enough to unsettle the foot. No two are quite the same. Their small irregularities do not obstruct the path. They call the walker into it.

Over the years, many have stumbled at the beginning, expecting uniformity. Most learn quickly. Some become frustrated. Others smile when they realize that the unevenness is part of the approach.

This man did not rush. He paused after each step, then repositioned his balance, then paused again. A few paces behind him, I walked in silence. He did not look back.

Near the top, he stopped altogether. I waited a respectful distance behind. After a while, he turned and spoke.

"Do you ever smooth the stones?" he asked.

"No," I said. "They remain as they were designed"

He looked up at the gate. The clouds behind it were just beginning to lighten.

"I thought I had made up my mind," he said. "But every time I take a step, it changes."

He looked down again at the steps beneath his feet.

"They feel like the way I'm thinking. Off balance. Nothing solid."

I said, "That is how these steps prepare the body. Not to carry certainty, but to walk with care."

He did not answer. But he turned and continued upward. His steps remained slow, but no longer hesitant. At the gate, he bowed with a quiet word of thanks. I bowed in return.

He entered the grounds alone.

I never asked what decision he was carrying. He did not return to speak with me. But that morning I was reminded of a truth I often forget. That the path is not made difficult to test us. It is made uneven to bring us back to attention.

In conversation, it is the same. We hope each step will follow the last in some regular rhythm. We listen with our conclusions already forming. We speak expecting the ground beneath us to stay firm. And yet each sentence may ask a different question. Each reply may change the shape of where we stand.

The man on the steps did not need answers. He needed footing. And that required presence, not certainty.

Some decisions ask only for movement. Others require uninterrupted silence between steps. The ones that matter most are rarely smooth.

Tomorrow, many visitors will arrive for the spring observances. Some will walk the stairs without noticing their irregular shape. Some will pause. A few will stop, as he did, and realize they are being asked to meet the way ahead with full attention.

There are paths that lead us outward. And there are those that lead us inward by asking us not to rush.

Not every unevenness is an obstacle. Some are invitations to place your footing fully in the now before taking the next step.

15

The Stranger in the Garden
What We See in Silence

There are visitors who arrive with questions, and others who arrive with silence. I once met a man who brought only the latter.

It was late one autumn. The maple leaves were crimson and the gingko trees glowed golden in the afternoon sun. The temple grounds had emptied of the last of the visitors and summer pilgrims. The paths were carpeted in leaves which crunched underfoot. Preparations for winter were underway: sealing the shoji panels against drafts, gathering root vegetables from the garden, storing the robes of lighter cloth. There was a quiet to the days that matched the calm in our practice.

While I was sweeping leaves on the path near the moss garden at the edge of the woods, I saw a figure standing in the shadows of the cedars. He stood motionless, gazing at the temple. He wore simple clothing, neither the robes of a monk nor the clothing of a typical visitor. His stillness was what caught my attention. It was not the momentary pause of someone admiring the view, but the rooted immobility of one who has found his place.

At first I thought he might be a traveler who had lost his way, or someone uncertain whether visitors were permitted so late in the season. I raised my hand in greeting. He did not respond. Not even a flicker of acknowledgment crossed his features. He simply continued his silent observation.

I returned to my sweeping, but my awareness remained partially with this motionless figure. The broom's rhythmic sound against stone seemed louder in the presence of this watching silence. When the sound of the bell for evening meditation filled the air, I lifted my broom and proceeded to the meditation hall.

Later, I told the abbot about the man. His response was simple: "He has not asked for anything. Let him be."

That evening, as the sun fell behind the mountains and the chill of the autumn night hugged the valley, he remained. He had moved closer to the temple grounds. A young monk said that the man had no pack and had not spoken. He now sat on the ground near the old camphor tree and looked toward the main hall. He was as motionless as the stone lanterns lining the paths.

Some of the monks looked troubled. We were accustomed to structured routine and order. To a known rhythm. This stranger did not fit.

One monk whispered that the man might be of disturbed mind. Another said he could be dangerous. A third thought he wanted to join the community but was afraid to ask.

We filled the silence with stories. We gave him a purpose, a reason, a role. We could not bear the emptiness of his presence. A man with no explanation.

The next morning, frost covered the grass and fallen leaves. It looked as if he had not moved at all through the night.

I noted how quickly we moved to ascribe an identity, a purpose, a narrative to this silent figure. How uneasy we were with the emptiness he presented. He was a person without a stated intention.

The monks went about their routine tasks, but I observed small changes in their activities. They took paths that kept them at a distance from the stranger. They glanced toward him as they worked. Some spoke in whispers in his vicinity, as though his silence expected silence in return.

I was alert to the stranger's presence in the way one is aware of storm clouds darkening the sky. Not immediately threatening, but heavy with possibility. I waited for him to come forward. Would he ask for food, or request shelter, or seek conversation? He did none of those things.

On the third day, as the morning mist moved through the valley, I approached him. He sat cross-legged, hands resting on his knees. His clothes were dusty from travel, his worn shoes streaked with mud. Though the morning was cold, he wore no outer garment. His eyes were open but unfocused, as though not seeing the temple before him but looking through it to what lay beyond.

I bowed with the customary greeting, in acknowledgment of his presence. He did not respond. I placed a small bundle of rice and pickled radish wrapped in a leaf on the ground nearby. He did not look at it. For a long while, I sat beside him. Not in inquiry. Not in welcome. Just to be there, sharing the silence.

The wind moved through the bamboo grove nearby, creating a delicate rattling sound like distant rain. Leaves scraped across the gravel paths. A crow called from the forest's edge. The man's breath was even, neither shallow nor deep, the breath of someone completely at rest within himself.

While I sat in this shared silence, I ceased to be concerned about his identity and motives. These questions were replaced by a different awareness. There was the rough ground beneath us. There was wavering light as clouds passed overhead. There were changes in temperature as the sun warmed the air. By evening, when I returned with water, he was gone. The food remained untouched.

Some of the monks were relieved. Others were curious. One asked if I thought he had been a ghost, or perhaps a manifestation of Kannon come to evaluate our hospitality. I said, perhaps.

He was not a ghost. He was a visitor without a story. He was a presence without an introduction. More than any appearance of mystery it was this that was disquieting. We assume that the people around us will tell us who they are. That they will explain their intentions and their identities. If they do not then we invent stories to replace the unknown. Confronting that man's silent presence, I found myself in dialogue with my own uneasiness. My mind sought to name him: wanderer, madman, fugitive, threat. But there was no evidence to ascribe any of these categories. I was left with my own projection resulting from my need to classify in order to understand.

The encounter with uncertainty is the most difficult challenge in resolving conflict. When we meet a person whose motives are inscrutable, whose behavior does not conform to our expectations, whose silence offers no basis for our understanding, we must then decide how to react.

Do we impose our story? Do we demand explanation? Do we retreat into suspicion? Or can we remain present with the unknown, neither reaching for hasty understanding nor retreating in fear?

For three days, our community engaged in this internal struggle. Some monks responded with wariness, creating physical distance. Others constructed explanations to make the stranger comprehensible. A few approached with offerings, attempting to establish a reciprocal relationship. Each response revealed the nature of the monk who offered it.

In our daily lives, how often do we engage in conflict with our image of the other? With our assumptions and fears? We believe we are responding to words, actions, and intentions, when we are reacting to the story we have created about who they are.

Resolving conflict must begin with the understanding that the person we face is a stranger who is unknown and unknowable. Even those closest to us possess depths we can never fully fathom. Their actions may be driven by motivations we cannot entirely understand. Conflict arises because we have filled the spaces of uncertainty with our own projections.

After the stranger's disappearance, the monks began to speak of their responses to his presence. One disclosed his fear. Another described his irritation at the interruption of routine. A third spoke of the tension between the responsibility of hospitality and the security of boundaries.

In sharing these internal struggles, they discovered how differently each had perceived the same silent figure. This is the heart of many conflicts. Not the objective reality of what has occurred, but the variety of ways we understand and react to that reality. Two people encountering the same event may construct altogether different meanings from it. A word spoken with one intention may be understood with another meaning. A boundary drawn for self-protection may be perceived as rejection. The most challenging conflicts are those in which we cannot even agree on the nature of what is being discussed. Encounters where our perceptions differ so fundamentally that we strive to identify common ground from which to begin.

About a year after the stranger's visit, late one afternoon, a traveler arrived at our temple. He was gray haired, perhaps in his late sixties, dressed in worn dusty clothing. In a subdued, halting voice he requested shelter. He told us that he had been walking a pilgrimage path to visit temples and shrines in the region. While in a remote forested area, he had developed a fever with dizziness and overcome with exhaustion, had collapsed on the side of the road. A man found him and carried him to a small one-room hut in the forest. He cared for him for several days until the fever broke. The man had not given a name or spoken more than a few words. He had mentioned our temple and suggested that it was a place where he could find rest on his journey.

The description of this man matched the stranger in our garden. This story, however, did not solve the mystery but heightened it. The stranger had not been lost or homeless. He had not needed help. For reasons known only to himself, he had decided to sit at the edge of our community, neither fully present nor fully absent.

The stranger mirrored each person's assumptions. Those who were inclined to be suspicious saw an impending threat. Those inspired by compassion saw the embodiment of suffering. And those searching for meaning saw spiritual purpose. It is as if, in his silence, each monk encountered his own reflection.

When our constructed stories and beliefs about the other are dismissed, a vast space opens for engagement. In this space we engage simultaneously with our counterpart and with our own need for explanation and resolution. One method to address such conflicts is to pursue clarity. Insist that the other precisely define himself and his intentions. This approach, which provides the comfort of understanding, closes the door to deeper connection. Possibilities existing outside our categories then become unreachable.

A more challenging path is to remain present with the unknown. Allow the other to be, at least for a time, undefined. Observe without interpreting. Wait without demanding. This path involves confronting our own discomfort. We must surrender to ambiguity. There are conversations that confront you with the inexplicable. A partner's unexplained withdrawal. A friend's uncharacteristic anger. A colleague's incomprehensible resistance.

When this occurs, observe your internal response. Are you creating a narrative to explain the behavior? What identity are you assigning? What motives are you attributing? It is as if you are meeting not only the other, but also a stranger within yourself.

Set aside your interpretations. Face the other as you would approach a stranger sitting silently at the edge of your garden. Can you express curiosity rather than conclusion? Can you meet him with presence rather than projection?

This requires the creation of a space for the other to be more than your explanation of him. It means recognizing that what seems to be rejection could be fear. What appears as anger could be pain. What casts the shadows of a wall of indifference could be uncertainty. In each meeting, there is an invitation to expand beyond the boundaries of your beliefs, to discover what is unfamiliar not only about the other, but also about yourself.

The stranger in the garden offered nothing. No words of wisdom. No insight. No instruction. Yet, in his silence, he revealed how quickly we move to frame the unknown. Self-discipline is necessary to allow the unknown to remain unknown long enough for a deeper truth to emerge.

In this he became a teacher.

16

The Listener's Path

On Entering the Other's World

There is a stone bench in a small city park I pass through each year when the weather begins to change. The grass is often worn from the summer's footsteps, and the earth smells of leaves already turning. The bench faces a fountain with no center, just many jets of water rising and falling in irregular patterns.

One afternoon, I sat there watching a man and a woman seated several paces apart on the edge of the fountain. They were close in age, perhaps partners. The woman spoke first. Not loudly. Her voice was even, but her hands moved as if tracing the outline of a thought she could not express. The man looked toward her but said nothing. His gaze lingered, caught somewhere between attention and retreat. With an expression of impatience, he began to speak before she had stopped. She adjusted her position, set her hands in her lap, and waited. When it was her turn again, she tried to clarify her meaning.

He was listening but not hearing. Looking but not seeing.

There is a pattern that arises in conflict, especially between those closest to us. The voice of the other becomes a terrain to navigate rather than an offering to receive. We begin to listen not for meaning, but for pause. We listen for the interval when we can begin to speak. And in doing so, we lose the thread. Not of logic, but of true attention.

To listen with presence is to allow everything else to fall away. The thoughts about what it means. The fear of where it may lead. The impulse to respond. All of it set down, just for a time.

All that exists is the voice of the other. Not only her words, but the cadence. The breath between sentences. The motion of the face when speaking words that carry weight. The shift in the shoulders when naming what has gone unspoken.

There is no rush to understand. Understanding will come.

There is no need to prepare. The reply will take shape when it is time.

What people most often long for is not agreement. It is to be seen without interruption. Heard without anticipation. Received without being managed.

When presence is whole, the other begins to unclench. Not because they are convinced, but because they no longer have to fight for attention. Their words do not fall into a void. They fall into the open hands of someone who is actually there.

In time, when the other has finished, there is a pause. Not out of politeness. Out of respect. A breath between voices.

Then the response begins not with defense or statement, but with acknowledgment. With words drawn gently from the voice that came before.

"You said this."

"This is what matters to you."

"This is what you want me to understand."

Not as technique. As truth.

Then, when the other feels heard, when their words have landed, the reply can rise from presence, not from position. Not to win. Not to protect. But to join.

No desire. No aim. No plan.

Just clarity. Just now.

Just one voice. And then another.

The next time you find yourself in an argument, notice your own listening. Are you hearing, or are you preparing? Are you receiving, or are you anticipating?

Set down your reply.

Let the other speak.

Watch the face. Hear the breath. And when the silence comes, let it be long enough to show that a new beginning has taken shape. Then speak only from where you are.

If you are present, your words will be too.

And if you do not reach for resolution, it may come to you on its own.

Like water in a fountain that needs no center to rise.

17

The Door That Opens by Itself
What Opens Without Force

There is a dream that returns to me from time to time. It arrives like mist drifting from the sea. In the dream, I am walking in the mountains. I do not know which ones. The air is thin and cool. The earth is yielding beneath my feet. Pines rise in tall columns along the ridge. There is no path. Only direction. I move uphill, without strain, as though the way had already been chosen.

I come to a cliff. Set into the stone is a door, not crafted, not framed, but there. It appears that the mountain itself had once parted and then slowly closed. There is no handle. No hinges. Only a faint seam.

I place my hand on the surface. I do not knock. I do not speak. I listen. The stone is cool with morning. I do not wait with expectation. I do not wait at all.

And always, when I no longer want it to open, it does.

There is no sound. The door does not swing. It is no longer closed. I step forward.

What lies beyond is not revelation. It is not emptiness. It is a clearing. Moss-covered earth. A single pine. A small stone, flat and dry, with a warm cup of tea resting on it. There is no message. Only silence. Only a sense of rightness. Of nothing more being needed.

And then I awaken.

In that dream, I never linger long in the threshold. But the dream stays with me. I remember it most in conversations that go nowhere. When words tighten. When understanding recedes. When everything that is said only seals the door more firmly.

In conflict, we often reach for explanation. We press forward with reasons. We believe that more clarity will loosen what is stuck. But some doors do not open through clarity. They open through presence.

I have sat across from people who do not want to hear me. I have watched their eyes narrow, not in anger, but in certainty. I have seen their breath shorten as they prepare their next reply. I listened without gathering. I stayed without learning. And slowly, almost imperceptibly, the tension eased.

Not always. Not quickly. But sometimes, what is fixed loosens when it is no longer being forced. This is neither about silence nor patience as a strategy. It is engagement without grasping or avoiding.

When we stop attempting to open the door, the space begins to breathe again. What was held in a crushing grip remembers its shape. Others may speak differently because the energy in the room has changed.

Presence is not intention. It does not involve forethought or tactics. It accepts. And at times, that acceptance opens the door.

The door in my dream does not open because of worthiness or wisdom. It opens because the struggle within me has quieted.

In conflict, we want to be heard. We want to be understood. We seek what benefits us. But beneath these desires lies a quieter truth. A more essential clarity. It is a clear seeing: *I am here. You are here.* We exist together in this breath, in this unfolding present.

When we stop arguing and become present, there is a change. What seemed like opposition fades. We realize we were hearing our own voice bouncing off closed walls.

We do not always need to be heard. We need to remain. And let what is true appear without pressure.

The door opens when we are no longer asking it to.

It opens when we are already standing on the other side.

18

The Burned Map
Trusting the Ground Beneath

Years ago, I was walking through the eastern foothills of the Hida Mountains. I had followed an old route north, guided by a small map that had been folded many times, and worn by age.

On the second day, I stopped at noon to prepare tea beside a small fire. I placed the map beside me on a low, flat rock. As I prepared tea, the fire popped, just once, and a small coal jumped out, landing near the paper. I turned too late.

The flame had already found its edge. I stood for some time, watching the last fragments lift and fall.

Then I walked on without the certainty provided by the map. I followed the sun and watched the slope of the land, the movement of birds, the line of water down the rocks. What had been a route became an unfolding. What had been a plan became a series of choices, each made without certainty.

I reached a village by dusk. There was no sign to mark its entrance. Only the smell of rice cooking somewhere behind a shuttered window.

I stayed there overnight. I said little.

Since then, I have often thought of the burned map with respect. It led me to the awareness that in conflict, we carry many maps. Maps of how the other should respond. Maps of what will happen if we say this or do not say that. We walk into conversations not only with language, but with routes already drawn in the mind. We are not embracing the immediate as it unfolds. We are following a plan.

And then the unexpected confronts us.

The other does not speak the anticipated phrases. We are misunderstood. We are not answered. The tone changes. The sky darkens. The map we had been relying on begins to burn.

What happens next reveals everything.

The mind panics. It tries to redraw the path from memory. It searches for where we went wrong. It wants to speak more quickly, to push harder, to get back to where we thought we were going.

But the path is gone.

And there, if we are willing, is presence. The presence of not knowing. The presence of being willing to stay without the story of what should happen next.

There is no route to certainty. There is only attention.

When we set aside the map, we begin to notice the land.

The edge in the other's tone that was not anger, but fear.

The silence that was not withdrawal but waiting.

The phrases we were about to say that had more to do with yesterday than now.

I am not suggesting that maps have no value. Preparation matters. But when conflict enters, the map burns. The current instant becomes unmapped. And we must walk it as it is.

Presence in conflict does not mean having the right language. It means listening without leaning forward. It means pausing not for effect, but for truth. It means allowing the path to appear beneath our feet, one step at a time.

The next time your conversation does not go as planned, do not reach for the old map. Do not rush to redirect. Do not demand the ground become what it was.

Remain where you are.

Feel the wind in the trees. Notice how the light changes. Let the fire burn what it must burn.

And then walk.

Not forward, not backward.

Just here.

19

The Quiet Meal

The Distance Between Intention and Perception

One spring evening, I was invited to dinner by a former student who had once trained at the monastery. His name was Kenji. He had practiced with us for some years, then left with apologies, choosing to return to lay life. There was no conflict, only the quiet step of someone recognizing his path.

He had written to me weeks before: "If you find yourself nearby, please allow us to host you for a simple meal."

My path did bring me near.

His home was in a suburb at the end of the train line. As I walked from the station, through narrow streets, the summer breeze carried the faint scent of wisteria.

Kenji met me at the gate with a smile and a bow.. He looked much older and moved with the same deliberate care that I remembered. After a brief greeting, he led me into the house and offered a place to sit while he prepared the meal.

I noticed signs of family life: shoes lined carefully, a calendar marked with school events, a bowl of over ripe fruit. There was an undisturbed quiet in the house. Not emptiness. Restraint.

When we sat down to eat, three places were set. His daughter, Emiko, joined us just after we began. She bowed lightly, offering the appropriate courtesies, and sat without speaking further. She appeared to be in her mid-teens, composed, inward, and slightly apart from everything around her.

Kenji did most of the talking. He asked after the abbot, the temple roof, the plum trees. I answered briefly. Emiko ate slowly, her eyes on her bowl. Once, when Kenji offered her more rice, she shook her head without looking up. There was no tension in her manner, but also no effort to be engaged in conversation.

It is easy to miss the fullness of silence. Two people may share a table and exchange a few phrases while inhabiting different realms. One may offer presence, believing it to be enough. Another may interpret the silence of that presence as absence. Intention and perception sometimes miss each other just enough to feel like distance.

After the meal, Kenji walked to the kitchen to prepare tea. Emiko remained seated at the table, her back straight, her hands folded in her lap. Then, she silently rose, glancing in my direction. "Excuse me," she said, gave a formal bow and left the room.

When Kenji returned carrying a tray with tea pot and cups, he hesitated and gazed at the table. "She speaks very little," he said. "Teenagers."

I said nothing.

He poured the tea into simple cups. It was slightly over-steeped, as if, lost in thought, he had let it sit longer than intended.

"She says little to me these days. Maybe it's the age. I'm away a lot for work and perhaps that's part of it."

He looked at the door then lowered his voice.

"She used to wait at the window when I came home. Now she's usually in her room. I don't know what she thinks of me."

He poured his own tea but didn't drink.

"I wanted this evening to be a reminder, for her or maybe for myself. A reminder that we're a family."

His words were neither sad nor bitter. Just uncertain.

We sat in silence as the tea cooled between us. Then he asked, almost reluctantly, "Did it seem like she was uncomfortable?"

I looked toward the table.

"She stayed," I said.

He tilted his head.

"She sat with us," I added.

He didn't speak, but his shoulders settled.

On the walk back to the station, I reflected on the space that lingered between the three of us at that table. It was not the space of chairs or distance, but a quieter divide, the space between intention and reception, between words spoken and meanings held.

We arrange meals, pour tea, and hope to light the room with our presence. But what we offer is not recognized as we hoped. Someone is sitting there asking, without words, to be seen in a way that no meal can express.

The space between people is shaped less by words than by the silence that follows. A kind gesture may be read as ritual. Presence can feel like absence when the heart expects a different kind of offering. And yet, Emiko stayed. She did not explain herself. She did not affirm the evening. But she sat, and she listened, and she bowed with customary formality. That was what she could give. It was enough if one could meet it without demanding more.

Many of our conflicts do not begin in anger. They begin in this silent space. They begin in the distance between intention and perception. We want to be received clearly, but we cannot always control how we are seen. And when our offering is not met as we expected, we begin to withdraw. Then the silence grows.

But not all silence is absence. It can be a way of staying. And it may be all that someone has to offer.

We cannot resolve every gap. We can only remain close enough that others may find their way back to us. Even when the tea cools. Even when no words come. Even when someone leaves the room before the cups are poured.

The Fallen Canopy
Embracing Changed Conditions

During the long night of the great typhoon, ancient trees bowed too deeply to the storm. The thunderous snap and splinter of boughs and trunks filled the meditation hall where we had gathered together for safety.

Just after dawn, as the winds began their departure, we left the hall to inspect the damage. More than two hundred fallen trees, many hundreds of years old, covered the grounds like corpses after a battle. Their trunks lay horizontal, root systems exposed to the air. Garden paths were covered with broken branches. The transformation was most striking in the moss garden.

For more than a millennium, the moss garden had flourished in an eternal jade twilight. The canopy of maples, cryptomeria, and pine had filtered sunlight, establishing the perfect conditions for moss to thrive. There were more than seventy varieties of moss some creeping along the ground in carpets of green, others forming small mounds like islands in a motionless sea.

But after the storm, the protective ceiling was gone. Sunlight flooded areas that had known only diffused illumination for centuries. The careful balance had been disrupted in a single night.

In those first days after the typhoon, many among us viewed this transformation with dismay. There was sorrow in the faces of those who had spent decades tending this garden. There was anxiety about what would become of the moss that had been carefully cultivated through generations. Some immediately began constructing bamboo shades to protect the most exposed areas, believing that human effort could and should restore what had been lost.

For weeks following the storm, the monastery was consumed with clearing debris, repairing damaged buildings, and replanting where possible. Some of the fallen trees were too massive to move. These were allowed to lie where they had come to rest, their decomposition now part of the garden's continuing story.

The bamboo shades did not protect the moss and blocked the air the moss needed. One by one, we removed them. Those who cared for the garden grew more concerned. Some said we should plant new trees immediately, although they would require years to grow. Their wish to bring the moss back revealed how easily attachment can resemble care.

One month following the typhoon, a small patch of moss was seen near a fallen tree. It was unlike the moss that had grown there before. Lighter in color, silkier in texture, it seemed to glow. In the weeks that followed, this new moss slowly began to spread. It appeared in other parts of the garden, always in the sunny spots where the old moss had died. It did not grow in the shade and seemed to thrive where the sun now touched the earth.

This new moss had not been planted by human hands. Its spores may have been present in the soil for centuries, waiting for conditions that would allow it to awaken. What had first appeared to be devastation had created the environment this species required.

Within a few months, there was a transformation. More than one third of the original moss disappeared. However, the garden was not fading; it was transforming. The new variety formed patterns shaped by the altered fall of light and shadow. Its color was vivid in direct sun and at certain times of day it almost appeared to glow.

There were other changes. Deprived of the dense tree canopy, bush warblers, woodpeckers, and green pigeons quickly disappeared. Skylarks, sparrows, and meadow buntings made new appearances. The insect population changed as shade-dwelling beetles and moths were replaced by butterflies and dragonflies. Even the sound of the garden changed. What had once been enclosed in silence now carried the sound of the valley stream. A garden once sealed within itself connected to the larger world.

The moss garden had not become better. It had not become worse. It had become what the new conditions required. This is a deeper form of harmony. We realized that rather than insist that reality match our vision, we needed to allow vision to arise from what is.

The traditional moss had not died out entirely. The moss continued to thrive where the canopy remained intact. Where there was partial shade, the old moss lived adjacent to the new moss. What had arisen was not so much a replacement as an integration. It was a new garden, not intentionally designed, but formed by a changed world.

In the life you share with others, there will be occasions when the canopy falls. A long-standing relationship may alter unexpectedly. The familiar tempo of communication may no longer hold. What once felt like a safe sanctuary may disappear in a single conversation, leaving light where there had been shadow and exposure where there had been security.

The first impulse is to restore what was, to return to the known. This response, although it may arise from love, can prevent us from seeing what new form the relationship might take.

Not every relationship can be refurbished like a damaged house. Some will evolve into a new kind of connection. The path is not to reestablish the old canopy. The Way is to nurture what is now taking root in the altered light.

A different kind of thought and awareness are required. The calm of observation is necessary rather than the pursuit of repair. Ask: What is fragmenting? What is emerging in its place? What was never viable before, but could be possible now?

What follows disruption will not resemble what came before. It may seem unfamiliar, even strange. At first there may be disappointment, or doubt. But if you can stay with what is becoming, if you can be patient with what has not yet revealed its shape, a new form of connection may take root.

The person with whom you speak after conflict is not the same person you knew before. And neither are you. The stories have changed. The narratives that have defined the other and yourself have disappeared. The question is not whether the connection can be restored. The challenge is to allow new growth to flourish in the open space where the old canopy once stood. When the protective patterns of belief or routine disappear, there is suffering in the exposure. But there is also the opportunity to cultivate a new honesty, compassion, and growth.

This is the work before us, not to force a design, and not to cling to what once was. It is to support what is beginning to grow now. To notice what can flourish in the light that has changed. To shelter what is tender but not shield it from every wind. To care for what is here, not for what we hoped would stay.

The moss garden after the storm is not the same garden. But it is still a place of life. The relationship that endures change is not the same relationship. But connection remains possible. Different in form. Perhaps even deeper in substance.

What is remembered is not erased. But alongside memory grows recognition. The new moss. The warbler's song. The way mist moves across the open space. There is elegant form here. Not in spite of change. But because of it.

21

The Pine and the Rock

Endurance Without Opposition

There is a black pine in the garden that leans against an enormous rock the size and shape of a breaching dolphin. The roots pour down the slope like streams of water. The trunk leans slightly to one side, yielding to what could not be moved.

Two of my cousins came to me, brothers rooted in the same soil, yet growing in opposite directions. Their family's soy sauce brewery had been handed down for centuries, like an heirloom too precious to discard yet too worn to be used as it once was.

One cousin stood firm in tradition: the *kioke*, the large cedar barrels, fermentation that spanned the seasons, recipes untouched by time. The other looked ahead with concern, warning that without adaptation, the company and its legacy would not survive. He spoke of stainless steel tanks, of shelf-life, and scalability.

When we sat together in the garden the silence was full of all they could not say. I listened as one might listen to a cliffside in the wind, the continuing echo of resistance.

I said little. Only this: "What is divided in anger does not easily reunite."

They returned some weeks later, out of formality rather than an expectation of successful mediation. I invited them to walk with me. The path curved through the garden, past the koi pond where fish swam in slow circles, past the stone lanterns worn smooth from countless years of rain. The red maple trees cast moving patterns of light across the path.

Then we arrived at the pine.

"This tree encountered a rock," I said. "The roots enfold the stone, and the stone supports the tree. Neither gives way, yet neither stands alone. Together, they have endured."

They were silent. One reached out and touched the bark, and the other knelt to study the curve of the trunk. Then we walked on. In that instant, a tension eased just slightly, like frost lifting from the edge of a branch.

Periodically we returned to the garden. Sometimes we walked. Sometimes we sat. Sometimes they spoke. Often, they did not. I listened to the silence between their words. This is where change sometimes begins.

In time, a way forward began to emerge. The traditional soy sauce brewing method would be maintained for their finest product, a tribute to what had endured. Meanwhile, a contemporary product line would be developed using more rapid fermentation techniques.

Each brother would walk the path he knew best. And each, in his own way, would rely on the other. The stone sat unmoved. The pine had not withdrawn. Yet in their immobile tranquility, a new shape had taken root.

When I see the cousins now, they may disagree, from time to time. But their voices have changed. They leave more space between their sentences. There is breath where there once was strain. They no longer try to straighten the other's trunk.

Conflict often creates the illusion of urgency. We are in a rush for clarity. We want our vision to prevail. But some impasses cannot be overcome. Growth is not always linear, and strength is not always straight.

Presence does not demand surrender, nor does it require appeasement, silence, or passivity. Presence is remaining rooted while staying open. It is rejecting the impulse to retreat or to conquer. Presence allows tension to exist without pressure to reduce it.

When in conflict, look to the place where you do not bend. Examine it not with judgment, but with curiosity. Then look again to the space around it. Notice what might grow.

Some rocks will not move. Some disagreements cannot fully resolve. Nonetheless, if we are willing to remain, a new understanding may emerge.

The pine is no less a pine because it curved. The curve is not the mark of defeat. It is the record of meeting resistance and continuing to grow.

You do not have to be straight to be whole.

You do not have to agree in order to remain.

You need only stay long enough to grow.

This lesson, like the tree, did not arrive all at once. It arrived through seasons, through calm spaces with those who carried conflict not as a sword, but as a burden to be lightened over time.

I have seen people divided by principle and pride, and I have seen others learn to lean just enough to hold.

The outcome is never certain. The tree may split. The rock may fracture. But if we stay, if we listen, if we release the need to prevail and simply remain, a new possibility may quietly unfold.

We may bend and not break. We may grow and not lose ourselves. There is an endurance that does not struggle or shout or demand. It listens. It stays. It leans.

22

The Last Few Steps

Leaving Without Closure

It was late spring, the kind of morning in which the air carries some of the night's coolness. The sun had not fully risen above the trees. The world was hushed, like a moment suspended between choices.

I had visited with my niece and her family for a few days. I had not seen her in many years. Not since her father's funeral. She sent an invitation after reading one of my letters. Her reply had been warm, but cautious. "Please visit if you like," she had written. "There is tea. And a room."

I had not expected to be remembered that way.

The visit was pleasant, measured, with occasional glimpses of warmth folded between stretches of silence that neither of us knew how to fill. Her children and husband maintained a distance and said little.

I rose early on the last morning. I was hoping to leave before anyone was awake. I had written a note to leave on the small table near the door. But she was already waiting in the kitchen, holding a cup of tea.

"You're leaving now?" she asked.

I nodded.

We sat at the table. I sipped tea slowly, and she did too, though hers had long since cooled.

After a time, she said, "It was strange having you here."

"Strange how?"

She shrugged. "It was like having a ghost in the house. Neither fully present nor completely absent. An unobtrusive and tranquil ghost. I thought it might feel more like when I was little," she said. "But it didn't."

"No," I said.

"You weren't really part of that time, were you?"

"Not closely," I said.

She looked at me over her cup. "Why not?"

I let the question rest for a few breaths.

"I thought it would be more helpful to step away," I said. "I thought the discipline I was learning would someday be useful to others. Maybe even to you."

She gave a small, tired laugh. "You left to help us?"

"I left because I believed in what I was doing," I said. "But yes, I also believed that my absence would have purpose."

"And now?"

"Now I see that absence has a truth of its own."

She looked down. There was no resentment in her tone. Only weariness. The kind that comes not from a single hurt, but the erosion of too many things not said.

She stood and rinsed her cup. I followed, placing mine in the sink beside hers. She dried her hands, then paused.

"I'll walk you out," she said.

We stepped outside together and walked slowly, without speaking.

"He asked about you," she said with an undertone of disappointment.

"I know."

"You never answered."

I didn't reply.

She stopped walking. I stopped too, beside her.

"You were like a myth to me," she said. "Someone who had chosen a higher path. I used to think that meant you had all the answers."

"I didn't."

"I know that now," she said. "But I didn't then."

I turned slightly to face her.

"You're angry," I said. "But more than that, you're disappointed. You thought I might return with clarity, with words that would make sense of it all."

She looked away, then back. "Yes."

"You wanted me to meet you, not with silence, but with truth."

"Yes."

"And now that I'm here, it feels like too little, too late."

She closed her eyes. "Yes."

We stood in the quiet that followed. There was no wind. Only a single bird call, brief and unreturned.

"I can't rewrite those years," I said. "And I can't offer the kind of clarity you hoped for. But I can say this: your words matter to me. Not because I need to explain. But because I want to understand."

She looked at me again, more gently now. "You don't need to fix it?"

"No," I said. "Not this."

We began walking again.

By the time we reached the road, her carriage had changed slightly, almost imperceptibly. Less braced.

She stopped where the pavement began and turned to me.

"You'll write?" she asked.

"Yes."

"About this?"

"If you'd like."

She thought for a heartbeat. "Just don't make it neater than it was."

"I won't."

We stood one breath longer.

Then she turned, and I watched her walk back up the path. She did not hurry. She did not look back.

Not every departure needs words to wrap it cleanly. Some leave a thread undone, not as failure, but as invitation.

Presence is not explanation. It is letting another speak until they're empty of waiting. It is replying not to defend, not to resolve, but to return what was heard. So, the speaker no longer has to hold it alone. And when we walk together, even partway, the past does not disappear. But it becomes lighter.

PART III
Embracing Difficulty
Remaining Open When the Path Narrows

23

The Ghost Boat
On Holding What Cannot Be Known

For thirty years, I have occasionally walked along a route that follows ancient stone steps down a cliff face, then follows the shoreline for a mile before climbing back to the temple grounds. It was an early November morning, when the Sea of Japan grows restless with the approach of winter.

On this particular morning, the familiar landscape was altered. In an inlet formed by two outcroppings of black rock, I noticed an object. At first, I thought driftwood had lodged itself between the stones, which often happens after storms. As I approached, I saw what I had not anticipated: a small wooden boat, its splintered hull wedged among the rocks.

The boat was six meters long with an open deck and small cabin structure. There was extensive damage from impact on the rocks. Faded Korean characters were visible along the bow.

I realized that I was facing what we had heard about in conversations with people from nearby villages. This was a North Korean ghost boat. For years, these craft had appeared along the coast. Although many were empty, some contained the remains of fishermen who had been unable to navigate home.

As I moved closer, I could see the outline of a human form inside the small cabin. The remains must have been in the boat for many months. There were bones partially covered by the remnants of clothing.

I bowed my head briefly in silent acknowledgment. Then I turned and made my way back to the temple.

The abbot was in the main hall. After I shared what I had found, the temple moved with simple purpose. The administrative monk placed a call to the local police. Two younger monks were assigned to lead the police to the site once they arrived. The abbot called a meeting of the senior monks.

"We have all heard of these boats," the abbot began. "Now one has found its way to our shore. While the authorities will manage the formal requirements, we must consider our own responsibilities."

Ishida, a senior monk spoke of how the person on this vessel had completed a difficult journey. Whether he sought to leave his homeland or was lost at sea, he had arrived where we might offer some measure of peace.

Watanabe, the administrative monk, always aware of our relationship with the local community, raised practical concerns. We must be careful not to overstep. This was a matter that involved international relations. The remains would need to be examined by officials; perhaps diplomatic channels would be involved. Our role must be appropriate.

A former maritime scholar who had joined our temple in middle age countered that we could not treat this as an administrative matter. He had spent years studying the currents of this sea. For this boat to arrive here -- the odds were remarkable. The person aboard had completed a final journey to a place of Buddhist practice. This seemed worthy of acknowledgment.

The discovery of the small wooden Buddha changed everything. When the police removed the remains, they had also catalogued the contents of a canvas bag found in the cabin: a spare shirt, some fishing line, and wrapped carefully within the shirt, a smaller pouch containing the carved figure.

"This cannot be coincidence," said Ishida, holding the police report. "A Buddhist fisherman, carried by currents across the sea, arriving at our shore."

Watanabe set down his tea cup with deliberate precision. "You are reading meaning into random events. Ocean currents are dictated by physical laws."

I felt the familiar tension building in the room. "May I offer a simple suggestion," I said. "We can have a *Sōgi*, a brief funeral ritual. We will chant the Heart Sutra, offer incense, and prepare a *kaimyō*, a dharma name, to recognize the fisherman's joining the Buddha's lineage. What matters is that someone acknowledges he lived, and that he is now received. Does this trouble you?" I asked.

"What troubles me," Watanabe replied, his voice measured but firm, "is that you are proposing to conduct funeral rites for a foreign national whose death involves international complications. This is not our responsibility."

"He did carry a Buddha statue with him," I said gently.

"It tells us that he owned a small carved figure," Watanabe spoke rapidly. "Perhaps it was a gift. Perhaps it was stolen. Perhaps it meant nothing to him at all. We cannot know."

Ishida leaned forward. "The currents that brought him here flow from the northeast, directly from the coast where these boats originate. For him to arrive precisely at our shore..."

"Is mathematically improbable but not impossible," Watanabe interrupted. "Ocean currents are complex. Boats arrive where they arrive."

I studied Watanabe's face. Behind his practical concerns, I sensed a deeper undercurrent.

"You seem particularly opposed to any form of memorial."

"I am opposed to unnecessary complications," he said. "We have relationships with local authorities, with the prefecture government. One misstep regarding North Korean matters and we become a news story. Our practice becomes secondary to politics."

"So, your concern is practical," I said.

"My concern is for the temple's wellbeing. And for avoiding actions that serve our emotional needs rather than genuine wisdom."

The words hung in the air. I felt their sting, but also their partial truth.

"You believe my desire for funeral rites serves my emotions rather than dharma?"

Watanabe's expression warmed slightly. "You saw this man's remains and feel moved to honor his suffering. That impulse is compassionate. But compassion without wisdom can create harm."

"What harm do you see in lighting incense for the dead?"

"The harm of assumption. We assume he was Buddhist because he carried a Buddha image. We assume his arrival here has significance. We assume we have the right to perform rites for someone whose beliefs and wishes we cannot know."

"These are fair concerns," I replied. "Yet he arrived at the rocks below our shore. The sea brought him to our coast. We happened to find him."

"You are determined to create a meaning that may not exist," Watanabe's voice gained an edge. "This is not a parable. It is not a teaching story. Why must we make it about us?"

The question stopped me. I felt its force, its uncomfortable accuracy.

"Perhaps," I said slowly, "because witness requires response. Because presence does not mean passivity."

"True," Watanabe agreed. "But response does not mean ceremony. We have responded with respect, with proper procedures."

"And if acknowledgment is not enough? If the Buddha figure suggests he would have wanted rites performed?"

"Why should we imagine the desires of the dead based on a small statue discovered in a foreign boat?" Watanabe asked. "That is not wisdom. That is projection."

The room had grown quiet under the force of his words.

"You raise meaningful questions," I said finally. "About assumption, about authority, about our motivations."

A middle-aged monk named Sato, who rarely spoke at meetings, cleared his throat. "Perhaps we should ask what the person himself would have wanted. We now know that he practiced Buddhism. Was he fleeing oppression or caught in a storm? We know nothing."

"Exactly," said Ishida. "We know nothing. But he is here. In this place. That must carry meaning."

"It means the current brought him here," Watanabe said flatly. "Nothing more."

The voices began to overlap. Tanaka argued for Buddhist funeral rites. Watanabe believed that non-involvement was the only appropriate response. Ishida spoke of spiritual importance.

I felt the familiar tightening that comes when good people hold incompatible truths. Each monk was right within his own understanding. Each was also incomplete.

The abbot finally raised his hand. The room quieted.

"What do you think?" he asked, looking at me.

I had been the one to find the boat. But I had no more answers than anyone else. Only questions and the reality of having seen those remains.

"I think," I said slowly, "that we are arguing about what to do because we have not yet sat with what has already happened."

Several monks frowned.

"A person died," I continued. "Not in theory. Not as a political issue. A human being experienced fear, maybe hope, certainly suffering. He drifted alone on the sea until he died. Then he drifted longer until he reached our shore."

I paused, feeling the attention in the room.

"We want to respond correctly. But perhaps we need to first receive what has arrived."

Tanaka looked confused. "What do you mean, receive?"

"I mean to sit with the reality of what happened without immediately deciding what it means or what we should do about it."

Watanabe leaned briefly, then straightened. "That sounds like avoiding responsibility."

"Does it?" I asked. "Or does it sound like not rushing past the actual experience toward a solution?"

The abbot raised his eyebrows slightly. "Continue."

"Each of you sees a part of the truth," I said. "Tanaka sees our duty to honor the dead. Watanabe sees our responsibility to act wisely within our circumstances. Ishida sees the mystery of what brought this person to us. Sato sees our ignorance about who this person was."

I looked around the room. "Perhaps all of these things are true at once."

"Then what do we do?" asked Tanaka, his urgency undiminished.

"We hold them all," I said. "We don't choose between compassion and wisdom, between meaning and mystery. We find a way that honors what each of you sees."

The room was silent for a heartbeat.

"That sounds like compromise," Watanabe said, but his voice had not lost its edge.

"Perhaps," I replied. "Or perhaps it sounds like completeness."

The abbot spoke for the first time since the discussion began. "What would that look like?"

"I had no prepared answer. But as I sat with the question, a quiet clarity began to form."

"The authorities will manage what is theirs to manage," I said. "That fulfills Watanabe's concern for appropriate action."

Watanabe listened without expression.

"And we acknowledge that a human being completed his final journey to a place of Buddhist practice. We offer recognition through funeral rites. That honors Tanaka's call for compassion."

Tanaka was listening intently.

"We accept that we will never know why this happened or what it means beyond the fact that it occurred. That satisfies both Ishida's sense of significance and Sato's recognition of our ignorance."

The room was quiet. I could hear the wind outside, the same wind that had carried the boat to our shore.

"Incense burned," I continued. "A chant of the Heart Sutra. An acknowledgment that someone who suffered has returned to emptiness. Nothing complicated. Just our presence."

The meeting room had fallen into a heavy silence. Watanabe's jaw tightened as if to hold back a deeper current of thought. He looked toward the window, the early winter light pale against the dark wood of the hall.

"I continue to say no rites should be performed," Watanabe said at last, his voice low but cutting. "We do not know what this man believed. We have no authority to decide."

The words hung in the air like smoke. I waited, watching him.

I said gently, "Sometimes we do not need authority to see what is before us. A man has died. He carried a Buddha with him."

"That means nothing." Watanabe's voice was tight. "Perhaps he stole it. Perhaps it was smuggled or planted."

"Perhaps," I said. "And yet, it was there."

Watanabe's hand closed into a fist against the table, then opened. His gaze remained fixed on a point far beyond the room.

"It's easy for you to speak of compassion," he said, his voice lowering almost imperceptibly. "You didn't lose anyone."

I tilted my head slightly, waiting. His words carried a gravity he had not yet named.

Watanabe's voice grew thinner, almost as if he spoke to himself. "My older brother was abducted by North Koreans on a beach near Niigata in 1982. My mother lit incense for him every morning, but it never brought him back."

"I did not know," I said gently.

The air felt heavier, the distant sound of the sea a faint murmur beneath it all.

After a breath, I spoke. "Perhaps this man, too, had someone waiting for him. Someone who will never know where he went or how he died."

Watanabe flinched, a small motion that barely broke the silence.

I added, "To offer a simple recognition may keep us from hardening into what we fear."

"There was a long pause. Watanabe inhaled slowly, then released the breath as if letting go of a weight he had carried."

"I'm not saying I agree," he said, his voice almost a whisper. "I'm saying I understand."

The conversation that followed became calmer in tone. Tanaka spoke of compassion. Ishida of the sea's strange currents.

The discussions continued for another hour, but the heat had gone out of them. Details were worked out. Concerns were addressed. Agreement emerged not through victory of one view over others, but through a recognition that the fullness of the situation required all perspectives.

The authorities documented the scene with cameras and notepads, two officers carefully examining the boat while another made phone calls from the pathway above. There was no dramatic police activity, just the efficient work of rural officers following protocol for what had become, unfortunately, a familiar procedure in some coastal regions.

They removed the remains, making the difficult ascent up the cliff stairs. They asked questions, recorded answers, and created an official account of what had happened before placing a simple notice on the boat indicating it was under investigation.

No public announcement was made, no local residents were involved. The complex history between Japan and North Korea made this a matter we approached with care.

In the weeks that followed, we learned fragments about the vessel and its occupant through conversations with the local police. The boat matched the design of those used by North Korea's state-controlled fishing fleets, vessels sent increasingly far from shore as government quotas increased despite depleted coastal stocks. The remains were those of a man, though little else could be determined with certainty given their condition after months at sea.

No identification was found. The cause of death was officially listed as unknown, although exposure and dehydration were the likely factors. After examination, the remains would be cremated and stored according to Japanese legal procedures for unidentified persons.

A few weeks after my discovery, when the authorities had concluded their investigation and had not yet dismantled the vessel, I walked again along that same rocky shore. The boat was there, although weathered further by winter storms. I thought about the fisherman. No family would claim him. No country would want him.

The wind tugged at my robe. I felt the cold on my skin.

I thought about the conversation in the meeting hall. How quickly we had moved to positions, to arguments about what should be done. How the reality of the person's death had almost been lost in our need to respond.

"But a subtle change occurred when we stopped trying to solve the problem and began receiving what had actually happened."

The tension in the room had changed. Not because anyone had won or lost an argument, but because the fullness of the situation had been allowed to breathe.

We are all shaped by the cultures into which we are born. The language we speak, the rituals we follow, the stories we inherit shape our days, our hopes, and our sense of who we are. They tell us what is proper, what is shameful, what is worth living for.

I was born into such a story. A small fishing village in Shakotan on the west coast of Hokkaido. A family that fished, that ate simple food, that spoke in quiet voices. Later, the monastery, an unbroken lineage stretching back more than a thousand years. The robes I wear, the chants I know, the rhythm of days shaped by meditation, bells, and sutras are all part of that culture.

The man in the boat had his own story. A different language, a different land, different perceptions. When he left his country, he stepped outside that story. All that he believed, all he had been taught, could not hold him anymore.

The sea does not know flags. The wind does not ask for names. The fisherman had drifted into the open sky of not-belonging. And although I bow as I was taught and chant sutras handed down to me, I, like the fisherman, have stepped outside.

Zen teaches us to let go of every story. To see through the illusion of self and other, temple and village, monk and fisherman. To release even the teachings themselves.

The robe, the sutra, the lineage, these too are stories. The man in the boat left his story. I have left mine. Are we so different? To leave a story is to step into emptiness.

That afternoon in the meeting hall, I saw more clearly. Presence does not belong to any position or viewpoint. It is what allows all positions to be held without conflict. It is what remains when the need to be right falls away.

The monks in that room were not wrong to hold their different views. The conflict was not a problem to be solved but a fullness to be received. When we stopped trying to choose between truth and truth, space opened for a deeper clarity to appear.

Presence does not repair what is broken. It does not explain what is inexplicable. It does not belong to any tradition. It is what remains when the path disappears. It is the quiet that holds what cannot be held.

In conflict, we often believe that someone must be wrong for us to be right. That clarity requires choosing sides. But sometimes the deepest wisdom lies in holding paradox without collapse, in allowing incompatible truths to coexist until a larger truth emerges.

The boat remains in my memory, as does the silence that followed our simple memorial. Both remind me that presence is not a practice reserved for formal meditation. It is what becomes possible whenever we stop rushing past what is actually happening toward what we think should happen next.

The ghost boat had brought us not just the remains of a fisherman, but an invitation to discover what lies beyond the stories we tell ourselves about who we are and what we must do. That was the most meaningful memorial of all.

The wind moved across the rocks. The water touched my shoes. The tide lapped at the boat's hull. The wood creaked.

24

The Jade Pendant
Between Invisible Boundaries

Boundaries surround us, some visible, others hidden. The bark that protects the tree. The shell that houses the snail. Each boundary serves its purpose: not to divide but to express the link between what lies on either side. There are boundaries that exist only in perception. They are invisible lines that may be more rigid than walls of stone or barriers of law.

Long ago, I journeyed to China to visit the Tiantong Temple. It was a memorable five day journey. China had begun to open its doors, but regarded foreign visitors, especially those with a religious purpose, with vigilance.

Our monastery had maintained a connection with Tiantong Temple for centuries. There had been a shared lineage that continues a transmission of teachings across time, boundaries, and wars.

Recently, texts thought burned during the Cultural Revolution had been discovered in a temple wall. There were ancient sutras with rare commentaries on key teachings. After more than a year of cautious correspondence, official approval was granted for a brief visit by one person only.

On the flight to Hong Kong, I sat at the window and looked down through the cloudless sky at the ocean. During the approach to Kai Tak Airport, through the clouds I could see a tangle of glass and neon. I traveled by bus through densely crowded streets, past market vendors to the Kowloon-Canton Railway station. The KCR train to Lo Wu was old, with wooden seats and windows smudged with fingerprints.

I stood for hours on the line at the Lo Wu border crossing, following others across the bridge into Shenzhen. The checkpoint smelled of boiled pork. My documents were examined with a frown but returned.

I could not find a seat on the train to Canton, now called Guang-zhou. It was crowded with families carrying bundles wrapped in cloth. Conversations in Cantonese and Hakka mixed with occasional phrases in Mandarin. From my cramped location in the center of the car I could not see the passing landscape.

Four hours later, I stepped out of the train into the chaos of Canton. Vendors by the dozens were selling steamed buns, peanuts, bottled drinks, cigarettes, handkerchiefs, and combs. I boarded another train bound for Hangzhou. That night, resting on the wood planks of the sleeper car, I listened to the rattle of wheels against rails and the hiss of steam. The train stopped at small stations: Hengyang, Wuchang, Nanchang. The smell of coal smoke drifted in when the doors opened.

In Hangzhou, I followed the slow movement of passengers across the platform. An official standing near the exit grabbed my arm. "Nǐ, guòlái," he said in Mandarin, his voice edged with authority. "You, Come here."

He led me to a gray door at the end of the platform. It was scratched and dented with patches of rust around the handle. Rusty hinges squeaked as he pushed it open. Inside, there was a strong smell of damp concrete and old cigarette smoke. The room was the size of a storage closet which may have been its original purpose. There was just enough space for the grease-stained desk and one wooden chair. A stack of paper was pinned under a chipped ceramic paperweight shaped like a carp. On a low shelf was an electric kettle; its spout stained with rust. The kettle's electrical cord trailed into a cracked socket. The room was illuminated by a single flickering bulb.

Without stepping into the room, he gestured toward the chair, "Sit there," he said in a flat voice. He left, closing the door behind him. I could hear sounds from the station outside: a murmur of voices, occasional shouts, the screech of a train arriving, the static filled announcements of a loudspeaker announcing departures in rapid Mandarin.

After about an hour, the door opened and a uniformed official stepped in. He wore the dark olive-green uniform of the Public Security Bureau. A row of brass buttons ran down the front of his tunic, polished but tarnished at the edges. His wide brown leather belt was cracked and worn. There was a holstered pistol at his right hip. His black shoes were scuffed at the toes, the soles thick. He shut the door behind him and sat down at the desk. For a few seconds, he did not look at me.

"Papers," he said as though giving a command to a trained dog. He glanced at the letter of invitation and flipped through my passport. When he looked up at me, his hard gaze was calculating.

"Purpose of visit to China."

"To visit Tiantong Temple."

"Who invited you?"

"The Abbot of Tiantong Temple."

He paused, looking at the letter again, his finger tapping the page, a measured rhythm.

"Why would a Chinese abbot invite a Japanese monk?"

"There is a shared lineage."

"That is not an answer."

"It is the truth."

His eyes narrowed, and a quiet menace took hold of his voice. "Falsifying documents is a serious crime against the People. Do you know what happens to those who falsify documents? To those who lie about their purpose?"

"I have not lied."

"You are wasting my time!" he shouted. He slapped the table with the palm of his hand. "You will be arrested. You will be imprisoned. Do you understand?"

"Yes, I understand."

He leaned forward. "You could disappear. Who would know? You are a foreigner. You are not welcome here."

I observed him quietly. I neither resisted his words nor acknowledged them as truth. They were expressions of his role and his training.

He sat back, studying my face as if searching for cracks in my composure.

"You are from a Buddhist temple in Japan. What do you do there?"

"I sit."

"You sit?" His tone carried disbelief, almost mockery.

"I meditate."

"What is the purpose of your visit to China?"

"To pay my respects at Tiantong Temple and learn what I can."

He gave a short, quick breath, half a snort, half a sound of dismissal. His voice rose expressing contempt.

"Learn what? How to be a parasite?" The air around us grew tighter with his words.

I sat quietly, my hands resting lightly on my knees, feeling the breath move naturally through my body.

"To learn how to meet the world without resistance," I said.

His eyes narrowed to slits.

"Your words are worthless. There is no time for sitting. No time for dreaming."

"Then I will sit peacefully," I replied.

His fingers drummed on the desk, a staccato rhythm of frustration.

"You monks," he said, his voice dropping low with increasing intensity, "you do nothing. You produce nothing. You sit in your temples while others work. We have no need for men who hide from the world."

I did not defend myself or the tradition. His words fell into the space between us like stones into water, and I let them sink without creating waves.

He studied me closely, searching for anger or fear. When neither appeared, his tone hardened.

"You sit there, accused of deception, of spying, promised imprisonment, and yet you show no fear. Why?"

I breathed slowly, my gaze remaining relaxed but attentive.

"Fear serves neither of us," I said.

A slight change passed through his bearing. He leaned back and his breath seemed to release a tightness inside him.

"You do not argue. You do not explain. You do not demand to see higher authorities or invoke diplomatic protection."

"There is nothing to resist," I said. "You are doing your work. I am answering your questions."

His hand moved absently to his collar, and for the first time I noticed a small glint beneath the olive fabric. His fingers found it without effort, a thin cord barely visible as it slipped below his uniform.

He caught himself touching it and quickly moved his hand away, but then, after a pause of internal struggle, he slowly drew out what was hidden there.

A small, jade pendant in the shape of a Buddha image was attached to a thin white cord. "I have worn this since I was eight years old."

"My mother kept a Buddha statue hidden in the back of a storage closet during the ten years of havoc." he said, his voice dropping to a whisper. "Late at night, when the neighborhood committees weren't making their rounds, she burned incense. She said it was a reminder that some things last longer than troubles." He paused thoughtfully for a moment. "These traditions" he continued, an edge returning to his voice, "are leftovers from the feudal past."

"Maybe they were both," I said.

He looked at me closely. "Both?"

"Yes. Both superstitions and a way of holding what could not be spoken."

"I never understood why she risked so much for it."

I watched him, letting his words settle. "Some things are not measured by risk," I said quietly.

His eyes searched mine and in that moment, I saw not the officer, not the interrogator, but a son who missed his mother. "She died when I was eight years old," he said, his voice barely audible. "I kept this." He held up the pendant, letting it catch the light.

"She gave you more than an amulet," I said.

"What does that mean?"

"The insight that some things are worth sustaining. Even in silence."

He picked up my passport and the letter of invitation. "There is a problem with your travel permission," he said, his tone now matter-of-fact. "Your visa authorizes a visit to China but not to a temple."

Here was the practical obstacle that had been there all along.

"I see," I said. What should I do?"

"Specific authorization requires additional forms and signatures. It will require at least one month of processing through different departments," he said.

"Then I can wait," I replied. "Or visit only what the visa allows and return another time."

He leaned back in his chair, studying me with what appeared to be curiosity.

"There is another option," he said finally. "A provisional cultural research exemption. It would allow limited access: one day only, no photographs."

"That would be most generous."

He watched me for a few breaths longer, then picked up his pen, the sound whisper-light in the transformed atmosphere of the room.

"I will make some calls," he said. "This will require several hours."

Late the following day, I arrived at Tiantong Temple. The rediscovered manuscripts were more remarkable than I had imagined. The exquisite calligraphy covered the yellow pages like the flowing ripples and crests in desert sand.

Forty years later, my strongest memory is not the wisdom of the old texts, but the memory of a small room where two strangers had discovered they were not so different. In that cramped room with its flickering light, presence reminded me that beneath our roles, uniforms and nationalities, we are all human beings trying to honor what we hold most dear.

25

The Unseen Root

Where the Trouble Begins

In early spring, the camellia on the eastern path began to lose its leaves. At first, just a few fell. But by the third week, whole branches had turned brittle, their leaves yellowed and dry.

One of the younger monks came to me, concerned.

"Should we cut the damaged branches?" he asked. "Maybe it needs more water."

I then crouched near the base of the plant.

"Look," I said, brushing away the upper layer of soil. Beneath the surface, the root was exposed and pale. The earth around it had become compacted. The rainwater was not reaching deep enough. What the camellia needed was not more pruning, but care at the root.

We often treat conflict the way this monk wanted to treat the plant. We see what is visible: raised voices, harsh words, silence between friends. We attempt to address the immediate symptoms. We explain. We correct. We debate. But the cause may lie hidden beneath the surface.

I once spoke with a lay practitioner who had become estranged from his sister. They had not spoken in several years. The argument that had broken them was about a shared inheritance, but as he spoke, I sensed a deeper tension beneath the words.

"She always interrupts me," he said. "She always assumes I don't know what I'm doing."

I asked, "When did that begin?"

He hesitated. "I suppose… it's always been that way. Since we were children. She used to speak for me when we were out with others. I hated it."

I said nothing. He looked down, then added, "I never told her that. I just snapped this time."

What broke between them was not caused by one disagreement. It had been growing for years, unnoticed. The fight was the visible damage. The root had been neglected far longer.

In many conflicts, what stirs us now often echoes a wound from elsewhere. What we see is often a late blooming. What was buried has been quietly waiting to rise and breathe. This is not always obvious. Sometimes the root is not even shared. It may lie in one person's old wound, carried forward unconsciously. A parent's voice, long internalized. A fear of being unseen. A memory of betrayal. These roots hide beneath ordinary soil.

To address a conflict, we must first stop treating the surface alone. Ask not only what was said, but what has not been said. Not only what happened, but what has been carried for too long without words.

Presence requires us to listen with more than our ears. To feel where the tension really begins. To ask what part of the other person is trying to protect itself.

Soon after the camellia began losing its leaves, we removed the top layer of soil and aerated the ground. We added compost and loosened the roots. New buds began to appear. The old branches remained bare, but from lower down, fresh shoots emerged.

The damaged part had not been saved. But the plant itself was not lost.

In human conflict, too, we cannot always restore what has withered. But we can nourish what remains. We can tend the unseen. We can create the conditions for new growth to emerge. When next you are embroiled in a conflict, pause. Before you devise an explanation or defense, ask yourself: What may lie beneath this occasion? Is there a deeper need? Perhaps an older wound, the forgotten root?

You may not find an answer immediately. That is all right. The work begins with the question.

Do not be quick to cut what is withering. Loosen the soil first. Give breath to the unseen. Wait, and watch. What blooms above often begins far below.

Unattended Bag

Staying in the Tension of Misunderstanding

It happened at a small coastal train station. One of those places with a cracked cement platform, a faded sign, and a single wooden bench under a metal awning. The train was late. I stepped away to ask for a train schedule at the ticket window.

When I returned, a middle aged man with a moustache was standing near the bench. He wore a dark blue suit, jacket unbuttoned, loosened yellow tie, white shirt. He stood with his arms folded, facing the bag.

"Is this yours?" he asked.

"Yes it is," I replied.

"I was about to report it. You should never leave luggage unattended."

His voice was flat but taut, like a string pulled too tightly.

"Thank you," I said. "I was gone for just a minute."

He didn't move.

"I thought it might be dangerous," he said. "You never know these days."

I offered another nod, slower this time. "I understand."

He didn't walk away. Rather, he looked me up and down with a gaze that was not quite hostile, but colder. Measured.

"Are you traveling far?"

"No," I said. I named my destination.

He glanced at the bag. "I almost said a word. Left like that, it makes people nervous. They tell us to report unattended items. Especially now. You've seen the news."

I said nothing.

He added, "No offense."

It wasn't a question.

I felt a small tightening in my chest. Not surprise. Not anger. A tension that lived between being suspected and being spared.

"He glanced at my robes, then toward the tracks. "What temple are you from?"

"Eiheiji"

He gave a small nod. "I see."

Silence again. A long one.

Then he added, "You can't be too careful."

I looked at him.

"No," I said. "You can't."

He watched me for another few seconds, then gave a single nod and turned away. He walked to the far end of the platform and leaned on the railing, staring toward the sea.

I sat down beside my bag and exhaled slowly.

There was no insult I could name. But it left a mark.

To be misread is not new. But it is different each time. This man had not summoned authorities. He had only looked at me through the narrow lens of suspicion and found enough uncertainty there to stiffen his stance. That was all. But, at the time, it was enough to disturb the silence inside me.

I could have explained more, but explanation is not always what truth demands. There is a space in such encounters where the impulse arises to shape how we are seen, to make ourselves acceptable. But presence asks for a different response. It asks us not to vanish. Not to shrink. Not to smooth the self into a version more pleasing to others.

You will be mistaken for another. You will be seen through another's haze of fear or the film of his personal history. You will feel the urge to correct his wrong perception, to pour yourself into a mold just enough to pass through untouched.

Simply stay with the breath. Let the discomfort arrive. Let it wash through you without resistance. Not to harden. Not to withdraw but to remain. Not every tension needs to be eased. Some are meant to be held without explanation until they pass on their own, like trains through dark stations late at night.

The Last Window

Conflict With the Dying

In the final weeks of his life, an old acquaintance asked to see me. We had not spoken in many years. Our paths had crossed, more than fifty years ago, during a period of teaching in Kyoto. He was a lay practitioner then, intelligent and proud, given to penetrating questions and well-prepared opinions. He admired the teachings but resisted the forms. In his words, "I liked the well but not the rope."

Our last exchange had not ended well. He had accused me of arrogance. I had responded without enough humility. There were truths on both sides, but little understanding. After that, we fell out of contact. The silence between us grew.

Then word came that he was dying. Pancreatic cancer, already advanced. A former student of his had written to me, saying, "He asked if you would come. He said there is a part of his life unfinished."

I arrived in the late afternoon. The hospital room was private, with a single window looking toward the western hills. The curtain had been pulled back. Pale light rested on the foot of the bed.

He was much thinner than I remembered. His face had taken on the hollow dignity of the dying. Breathing was slow but even. His hands lay on top of the blanket, one curled slightly, the other open.

He opened his eyes as I stepped in. I bowed, offering customary formal courtesies, and walked to the chair beside the bed without speaking further.

We did not speak for a long time. The beeping of a monitor marked the passage of seconds. Outside the window, clouds drifted across the hills.

Finally, he said, "I wasn't fair to you."

I did not answer.

He coughed, then continued. "Back then. I spoke as though I knew more than I did."

I nodded once, slowly.

"And you," he added, "hid behind that silence of yours."

He turned his head slightly. "That made it worse."

I took a breath.

"You're not wrong," I said.

His lips twitched, almost a smile.

"I thought you might argue," he said.

"I used to," I replied.

He closed his eyes. The silence returned.

There was a presence in the room now that had not been there before. Not resolution. Not warmth. Only a quiet that left things unresolved. The old conflict still existed, like sediment at the bottom of a clear bowl. But it no longer stirred.

He opened his eyes again.

"Do you think we carry unfinished things into death?" he asked.

"I don't know," I said. "But I think we carry them while we live."

"And what if we don't finish?"

"Then we meet what remains."

He exhaled and looked back toward the window.

"I always thought the practice was about release," he said. "But maybe it's just about staying."

I said, "That may be the same thing."

He grew tired then. His eyes closed. I watched the rise and fall of his chest, the small twitches in his fingers. There was nothing more to say, and nothing that needed saying. He had fallen asleep.

I remained a while longer.

Then I stood and bowed toward him silently, low and full. He did not stir.

Then I turned and walked out.

I did not expect to see him again.

Two days later, a note arrived at the temple. It was brief. Not in his handwriting. A few words only.

"He said thank you. And he said you didn't need to respond."

There are many kinds of conflict. Some are heated, immediate, full of words and fire. Others are subdued, like fault lines beneath the ground. We step over them without noticing, until one day they rise.

The conflict between us had never erupted. But it had calcified from retreat. He had wounded with words. I had wounded with withdrawal. In Zen, we speak of meeting experience without resistance. But sometimes what appears to be calm is the absence of courage.

What does it mean to remain present with someone who is dying, when a wound between you has not been healed?

It means entering the room without defense.

It means not polishing the past.

It means letting silence say what words could not.

Not every conflict can be resolved. Not every wound will be closed with words. But presence does not depend on perfect repair. It depends only on the willingness to remain.

When someone you have not reconciled with is dying, you may feel the urge to fix, to confess, to be forgiven. But the greater act may be only to sit. Not to claim what was right or wrong. Not to relive. Only to be there as the final curtain is drawn.

Do not expect answers.

Do not wait for peace to be declared.

But do not turn away.

Sometimes the last window is not an instance of clarity, but a small opening of the heart. Just wide enough for the breath to enter. And leave.

I think of him now, sometimes, when I pass the hills at dusk. The light at that hour carries a quiet longing, unresolved and incomplete.

He asked if we carry the unfinished with us.

Perhaps.

But what we meet fully, even without resolution, loses its grip.

The last thing he said was that I did not need to respond.

This is my response: To sit with what remains; to meet the breath in front of me, without correcting the past; to stay, when everything in me once longed to leave.

The Train to Toyama
Remaining Present When Nothing Can Be Said

On a quiet weekday afternoon in early winter, I was on a local train bound for Toyama. I had boarded at the beginning of the line, heading back from a short trip. The train was mostly empty, a few schoolchildren murmuring near the back, an elderly couple with a thermos of tea, a suited man asleep.

I took a seat near the middle, placed my bag on my lap, and let my breath settle. The rhythm of the train. The blur of passing rice fields. I began to feel again the shape of silence I had held during the morning's meditation.

At the next station, a man boarded.

He was disheveled, face tight, clothes askew, a bandage on his wrist. He stumbled slightly as the train pulled away, then moved down the aisle. When he passed my seat, his eyes locked on mine.

He stood a moment too long, then sat across from me. His face twitched as he looked me over.

"You think you know." he said.

I said nothing.

"You sit in temples and drink tea. You don't know anything."

His voice rose slightly. The children in the back stopped talking.

"My wife left this morning. After twelve years. I didn't even hit her this time." He barked out a laugh.

The silence around us thickened.

He leaned forward, eyes sharp. "Come on, monk. Let's hear you talk."

I took a breath. I didn't look away.

"I'm sorry you're hurting," I said.

He sneered. "That's it? That's all your wisdom?"

I did not move, nor did I answer immediately.

"I cannot change what brought you here," I said slowly. "But I can stay."

He stared at me for a long moment. Then his jaw trembled.

"I haven't slept in two days," he muttered. "I keep seeing her pack the bag."

"I can stay," I repeated. "Until your stop. If that helps."

He looked away. His breath slowed. The train rocked on.

When his station came, he stood without a word. As he stepped off, he turned back, just slightly, and gave a small bow.

Then he was gone.

No resolution.

Just a moment.

Pain can live inside a person like heat beneath the skin. Not every wound needs a word. Sometimes what matters is not what we say, but whether we are there when nothing can be said.

Not to solve. Not to fix. But to remain.

Even a train can be a zendo. Even silence can meet suffering. Even presence can reach where explanation cannot.

Obaachan's Garden
Tending What Cannot Be Held

Many years ago, I returned to the village where I grew up. Ojiichan and Obaachan, my grandfather and grandmother, raised me after my parents died. The village looked like a miniature version of my memory. The houses were smaller, the harbor narrower, the surrounding mountains less impressive.

Ojiichan, had died long ago. But Obaachan continued to live in the one-story house overlooking the harbor. She had reached her ninety-second year. Her stooped figure was like a bamboo stem after heavy snow. Her hands, once able to mend fishing nets with astonishing speed, now quivered when she lifted her tea bowl.

Since before I was born, Obaachan tended a garden unlike any other in our fishing village. While most households grew vegetables in neat, practical rows, Obaachan's garden combined usefulness with an arrangement of stone, moss, and carefully placed plants that transformed the small plot into a place of unexpected beauty. It was a garden one could walk through slowly, finding new angles of sky and sea with each turn. Village children would sometimes stand at the low wooden fence, watching as she worked among plants arranged to echo the shapes of the surrounding coastline.

Ojiichan had built the house, but it was Obaachan who shaped the space that transformed shelter into sanctuary. When I was a child, I would watch her work in the early morning as she arranged plants and stones gathered from the shores. In her garden design she captured the special qualities of our coastal landscape. She worked with the intensity of someone performing a ritual that had meaning beyond its apparent outcome.

"The garden is not ours to control or bend to our will," she would say when I asked how she knew where each element should be placed. "The wind, the soil, and the plants whisper to us and we must listen. They will tell you where they belong."

A young fisherman drove me from the station and helped me with my small bag. He motioned toward the garden. "The old woman's garden," he said with respect, "People would walk up from the harbor to see it."

I understood what he meant even before I approached the gate. The garden was no longer as it had been. Winter storms had dislodged the stones Obaachan had arranged with precision. The plants that once thrived under her care were now stretched and thin. And the small maple, brought back years ago by Ojiichan from a journey to the south, had grown untended, its branches reaching out in all directions.

Obaachan greeted me at the door, her face brightening upon seeing me. We bowed to one another, a gesture as natural as breathing and then, without a word, we stepped into a brief embrace.

That evening, I cooked rice and the fish a neighbor had brought. Obaachan sat at the low table watching me with a combination of inquisitiveness and discomfort.

"Have you seen the garden?" she asked.

"Yes," I replied without comment.

"These hands," she said, holding them before her. "Have forgotten what they once knew."

I noticed how the joints had swollen, and the skin had grown thin and was marked with the dark spots of age. "The garden tools, the nets, the hooks have become strangers to me."

In her words I understood what some temple elders experienced. A disconnection between the tasks that must be accomplished and what the body will allow. It is a manifestation of suffering not often acknowledged in the teachings. A forced surrender of capabilities.

"I will spend some time in the garden tomorrow," I said. "As the season changes, the garden will change with it."

She stared at me with sudden intensity. "The garden belongs to the wind and rain. It does not need your temple ideas."

"Not temple ideas," I said. "Just hands."

The next morning, I stepped into the garden before dawn. The scents of the sea, pine and damp earth evoked memories of my childhood. Obaachan was sitting on the weather worn wooden bench facing the garden. She did not turn as I sat beside her.

"This is the best time for gardening," she said. You can hear the garden and the sea murmuring to each other."

The growing light revealed the heart of the garden and its neglect. Some of the larger rocks suggested the coastal boulders that had sheltered fishing boats for generations. The small stream diverted from the mountain spring flowed through carefully arranged stone channels. The pine, its form shaped by decades of sea wind as much as by Obaachan's hands, bent gracefully away from the sea.

"I will work here today," I said. "Tell me about the plants I may not recognize."

She was silent for a time. When she finally answered her voice carried the hard edge I remembered from childhood scoldings.

"You think you understand this garden because you played in it as a boy. But knowing a place is not the same as knowing its nature." She turned to look at me directly. "Your temple gardens are different. The stones and plants do not speak the same language here by the sea."

I recognized the resistance in her words. For her, my gesture was never just about the garden. It revealed a turning of the tide between us. What had once flowed from her hands without question now returned in a form she was being asked to receive.

"Then I will listen first," I said. "And do nothing until the garden and sea have spoken."

I observed a slight relaxation of her shoulders suggesting that I had found the right response.

That day, I moved slowly through the garden. I observed how the sea wind interacted with each plant. How the changing light accentuated particular aspects of stone arrangements. I listened to the flowing water as it found its path through the rocky passages cut into the soil. I observed which plants had withered under neglect and which had flourished with less intervention.

Obaachan watched from the bench. Her gaze followed me with a wary optimism. Sometimes, she would call out brief observations: "That type of grass has always grown better closer to the wall" or "The large boulder is intended to be Takarajima."

At dusk, I returned to sit beside her. "Tomorrow morning," I said, "I will clear the stream channels. The sound of water is important."

She looked surprised that I remembered that the garden was planned for the interaction of sound, scent, and sight. The small stream, guided by carefully placed stones, created a counterpoint to the harbor's deeper rhythms.

"Yes," she agreed. "The voice of the stream is vital"

The next day, I cleared debris from the channels, enabling the stream to recover its voice among the stones. I removed those plants that had encroached too far into the garden path. But I deliberately left some that harmonized with existing elements.

Obaachan sat on the bench watching in silence for nearly an hour. Finally, she spoke.

"You are not doing it as I would have done."

"No," I agreed. "I cannot be your hands."

"Yet you are not making it into a temple garden either."

"No," I said. "I am listening for what wishes to emerge now, between sea and mountain, between what was created and what has been transformed."

She recognized the echo of her own teachings from decades earlier and her bearing softened.

"Perhaps I should join you," she said. "Not to work. But to remind your hands of what they have forgotten."

"I would welcome that," I said.

A daily schedule emerged. Each morning, I worked in a different area of the garden. I placed Obaachan's bench where she could observe my efforts. She gave orders. Sometimes I would follow her directions precisely. However, sometimes I pursued an alternative approach.

The result was neither her garden restored, nor a new garden created, but a third reality expressing the history of what she had created and current circumstances.

As the days passed, our interactions changed. Obaachan's directives became suggestions. A rhythmic routine developed that required fewer words. There were more shared silences.

One evening, as autumn's chill required the charcoal brazier to be lit, Obaachan surprised me by asking about my life at the temple. In my early monastic years, she had shown polite indifference to my spiritual practice. Her focus was the tangible world of sea and garden.

"Do you miss the monastery?" she asked. "The predictable certainty of temple bells marking time. The knowledge of what each day will bring?"

"There is less certainty than you imagine," I replied. "Each day offers its own unexpected turns, just as each tide brings different gifts and challenges to shore."

"Like a garden by the sea," she said.

She studied the glowing charcoal before speaking again. "When you were small, I thought I was teaching you about survival. How to read the weather, mend nets, tend plants that could withstand salt and wind."

Her voice reflected no sadness or regret. Only a thoughtful assessment of what had transpired between us. "I did not know that I was also teaching you how to care for my garden when I could no longer care for it myself."

"You taught me to listen to what emerges between sea and shore," I said. "That wisdom serves in all circumstances."

During my final days in Obaachan's garden, we finished the most important garden work together. Not every area received the same attention. We made decisions about what could be maintained and what could thrive without care. The resulting garden was neither a restoration of its former state nor a relinquishment of its character. It was, rather, an expression of a present reality that respected its history without being limited to it.

We sat again on the bench during my last morning. The mist rose from the harbor. The maple had surrendered most of its leaves.

"The winter storms will come soon," Obaachan said. "The garden will need attention again in the spring."

It was observation and invitation.

"I will return in the spring," I said.

As the silvery fog floated in from the sea, I noticed how our roles had reversed. I was now the one tending the garden, and she had become the watcher. But more than roles had changed. Between us, a quiet transformation had taken shape. The garden was no longer a gesture of giving from one to the other. It had become a shared rhythm. A collaboration. A care that moved in both directions. Not giving and receiving but shaping a mutual attentiveness rooted in the present.

When familiar roles begin to realign, between grandparent and grandchild, or in any close bond, what remains is not the role itself, but the regard that flows beneath it. In a relationship shaped by time, resistance brings pain. Nature resists nothing. Bamboo bends in the wind, the river flows around the rocks in its path. What may appear to be surrender is the presence to adapt to what is.

Harmony is not born from control but from seeing that change calls for new forms of connection. The garden Obaachan and I cared for belonged to neither of us entirely; it existed in the shared space between us. Much like a tree that bends rather than snaps in the wind, we found strength and resilience by learning to yield.

The most meaningful conversations are not about persuasion or instruction. They unfold between us, shaped by what is here. Between sea and shore. Between memory and change. Between the wisdom that endures and the humility to meet the present as it is.

In Obaachan's garden, I saw that care is neither command nor submission. It is presence. An attentiveness that honors what has been while remaining open to what is needed now. Sometimes that means preserving. Sometimes, allowing change. Impermanence and continuity do not oppose one another. They move together.

Each autumn the maple lets go of its leaves, yet it remains itself through winter's bare silence. The river may discover a new course after a flood, but it continues its path to the sea. Though Obaachan no longer prunes the branches with her own hands, her way of seeing shapes the garden. What seems like loss may carry continuity in another form.

Care must evolve as life does. What begins as giving becomes receiving. What becomes receiving transforms into mutual exchange. Each phase calls for a different kind of presence. Yet through all these changes, care remains what it has always been: the recognition of value beyond usefulness. In that recognition, we open to a space where life renews itself, not as we expect, but in forms we may slowly learn to receive.

First Light

What Cannot Be Fixed Can Be Met

He arrived just after dawn, unannounced.

I was sweeping the stone path near the south gate when I saw his figure in the mist, tall, tense, moving with a purpose he hadn't quite decided on. I recognized him before I could recall his name.

He had once been a novice here. Thirty-five years ago, maybe more. He had stayed for only a year and then left in the middle of the night without speaking to anyone. His *shikibuton* had been empty by morning. Folded robes. A copy of Dōgen's *Shōbōgenzō*, marked with questions he had never asked aloud.

I set the broom aside. He bowed low offering formal courtesies. I returned the bow with similar formality.

"Do you remember me?" he asked.

"Yes."

"I shouldn't be here," he added. "But I didn't know where else to go."

I gestured toward the stone bench beneath the pine. We sat. The light was low; the cold spring air settling on the skin.

For a long time, neither of us spoke. He sat as if waiting for the right shape for his words to arrive.

"I left angry," he said at last. "Angry at the rules. At you. At myself, mostly."

I listened.

"I told people later that the place was too rigid. That Zen was hollow. That I had seen through it."

He paused. I could feel what was coming before he said it.

"But that wasn't true. I left because I was afraid. I was afraid of what it showed me about myself."

He looked down at the dried pine needles covering the ground as if expecting judgment.

I said, "You are here now."

He laughed with sadness in his eyes.

"My brother died last month. Heart failure. No warning. We hadn't spoken in years. Last time we did, it ended with shouting. I said things I hear at night."

The breeze stirred the pine branches above us. The broom rested where I had left it.

"I thought if I came back here, maybe I could find a way to help. Some clarity. A way to let go of what cannot be fixed."

We sat in silence. A pair of crows called across the morning fog.

I said nothing.

After a while, he spoke again. "You know what's strange? As I sit here, I feel as though I don't have to explain myself anymore."

"You don't," I said.

"Do you think I'm too late?"

I looked directly at him. "Presence is not measured in years. It is measured in whether we turn away."

He exhaled through his nose, as if releasing a shadow he had carried a long time.

"I thought I needed to make things right," he said. "But now I'm not sure what right means."

The light had brightened. The mist was beginning to lift. The shape of the path returned.

"Some things are not right or wrong," I said. "They are just unfinished."

He looked at me. "Then what do we do?"

"We meet them."

He stayed until the sun cleared the trees. Then he stood, offered formal words of departure, and bowed.

31

Hospital Vigil
The Practice of Presence

Many years ago, I visited a hospital ward each day for three weeks to keep vigil beside an old friend and fellow monk. Perhaps from decades of inhaling incense in poorly ventilated temple rooms, his lungs had weakened. The rhythmic beeps of the vital signs monitor and the mechanical hiss of the ventilator produced a monotonous harmony as though the machines were chanting their own special sutras. My friend's palms rested motionless atop the thin blanket, fingers twitching slightly, as if remembering an unfinished task.

He had asked me to come, and I came.

The hospital was at the foot of the hills near the eastern edge of the city. From his fifth-floor window, I could see the distant mountains where our temple rested, though he could not. His bed faced a beige wall adorned with a television. The floor was gray linoleum worn thin near the doorway where countless feet had entered and exited.

The chair where I sat was molded blue plastic with a thin cushion that flattened entirely by midmorning. I would settle differently every hour or so, less from discomfort than from habit. In the meditation hall we did not sit longer than forty minutes without walking meditation between periods.

Early the first evening, a young nurse arrived displaying brusque efficiency. She glanced at the monitors, adjusted the IV, and asked me to move aside without glancing at my face. I moved my chair to give her space.

Her eyes on the monitor, she asked, "Are you family?"

"No."

"Only family can stay overnight," she said abruptly.

I nodded, neither agreeing nor disagreeing.

When she left, I remained.

A different nurse arrived later that evening. She was older, her gray hair pulled back from a face lined by years of night shifts. She placed a blanket at the foot of the bed. Then she brought a second blanket and placed it on my lap without comment.

"Night shift starts at eleven," she said. "The supervisor doesn't do rounds until two."

She dimmed the lighting and left. I understood what she had indirectly said. I could remain through the night if I were unobtrusive. This was the first instance of wordless dialogue. Unspoken and kind.

On the morning of the fifth day, a doctor arrived with three residents in white coats following like ducklings. He spoke in the language of numbers: oxygen saturation, white blood cell count, lung capacity. The residents took notes. None of them looked at my friend's face, only at the parts of him that could be measured. The doctor noticed me in the corner.

"You should step out during rounds," he said.

I remained seated, palms folded in my lap. The doctor hesitated, then continued his recitation of numbers. When they left, a resident glanced back at me with a curious expression.

The next day, I arrived to find the television on. A game show was in progress. The sound was harsh and loud after the pre-dawn tranquility of the temple where I had begun my morning. I located the remote control and turned it off.

An hour later, a different nurse entered and turned it on again.

"Most patients like a bit of distraction," she said helpfully.

"He has lived in temple serenity for sixty years," I replied.

She looked at me, then at him. "I didn't know," she said, and turned it off.

That afternoon, she posted a small note beside the door: "No TV please. Patient preference." It was the second instance of mutual understanding. Direct but simple. A small territory of calm was established.

The most difficult hours came during shift changes. It was a transitional period when information was exchanged, responsibilities transferred.

Conversation filled the hallway, some hushed, some loud. Carts clattered past. A phone rang somewhere, unanswered. Inside the room, the machines continued their duet of beeps and hushes.

Each day, I brought his *zuhatsu*, his black lacquerware rice bowl from the monastery. Each morning, I would place it on the windowsill where it was brightly illuminated in the early morning radiance. The bowl established a focal point which drew the eyes away from the machines. One of the nurses asked about it.

"It is his rice bowl from the temple," I explained. "For a great many years, he has used this bowl, never taking more than needed."

After that, each time she arrived, her gaze would linger on the bowl framed by the window like decorative art. A small bridge had been formed between our worlds.

On the eighth day, my friend's respiration became more labored. The numbers on the monitors flickered and fell. An alarm sounded and the room quickly filled with staff. Someone pressed a button on the wall. Someone else checked pupils with a small flashlight. A third adjusted medications through the IV line.

I moved to the corner beside the bathroom door, neither leaving nor interfering. A young doctor turned to me.

"You must wait outside," he said.

Our eyes met. He began to speak again and then stopped. There was an interval of calm between us. An unspoken exchange of understanding about authority and territory. He turned back to his patient.

That evening, the room hushed again, the older nurse with the gray hair returned to monitor vitals. She glanced at the corner where I sat.

"You were here during the code," she said. It wasn't a question.

"Yes."

"That's unusual. Most people can't manage it."

"I have sat with dying monks before," I said. "In our tradition, we do not turn away."

She adjusted a pillow with practiced palms. "Neither do we," she said. "But we have different methods."

"Yes," I agreed. "Though perhaps the same intention."

She looked at me directly for the first time. "Perhaps," she conceded.

The air between us altered quietly. It was a recognition across different disciplines, different approaches to the same experience.

The next day, she brought a new cushion for my chair.

By the second week, small changes had appeared in how the staff entered the room. Many would hesitate at the threshold, as if adjusting their internal rhythm before stepping inside. Some lowered their tones without being asked. A few would acknowledge me with a slight nod, neither approval nor disapproval, simply recognition of my continued presence.

I had not complained. I had not demanded. I had not lectured anyone about proper atmosphere for the dying. I had simply remained, embodying an alternative way of being with illness and impermanence.

The young resident who had glanced back at me began to linger for an interval after rounds, watching how I sat, how I attended.

"Are you meditating?" he asked on the twelfth day.

"Just sitting," I replied.

"What's the difference?"

"One has a purpose. The other is simply presence."

He considered this. "We're taught to always have a purpose," he said finally. "A diagnosis, a treatment plan, a goal."

"A worthy approach for many circumstances," I acknowledged.

"But not all?"

I gestured to my friend in the bed, to the machines, to the monitors with their flickering numbers.

"Has your purpose made space for his experience?"

The resident did not answer immediately. When he left, his steps were measured, more deliberate.

On the fifteenth day, a specialist arrived from another hospital. He spoke rapidly about experimental treatments, statistical outcomes, aggressive interventions. His energy filled the room like smoke, making it difficult to exhale. When he finished his recommendations, he looked at me.

"Are you the one making decisions?" he asked.

"No one is making decisions now," I said. "Only witnessing what is already happening."

He seemed confused by this response. "There are options available," he insisted.

I looked at my friend's face. The hollowed cheeks. The bluish tint to his lips despite the oxygen. The skin drawn tight across his cheekbones. I had watched him rake the stone garden at the temple, his back straight despite his eighty years. I had heard him chant the sutras, his tone unwavering through the night vigils. I had seen him sit in meditation through winter cold that frosted his eyebrows white.

"What do these options offer?" I asked.

"More time," the specialist said.

"For what purpose?"

The specialist's expression changed, his certainty faltering for an instant. He looked at the patient, perhaps seeing him clearly for the first time, not as a collection of failing systems, but as a person completing a journey.

"That's not a medical question," he said finally.

I agreed. "No, it is not."

Experimental treatments were not added. This exchange, brief but necessary, had introduced the act of seeing beyond the reflexive drive to extend life without asking why.

Three days later, before dawn, my friend's respiration changed. The machine continued its mechanical rhythm, but his body had found its own cadence. More gradual and less regular. I moved my chair closer to the bed. I placed my palm near his. Not grasping, just adjacent, the way river stones rest against one another after years of the same current.

The night nurse entered to check the vitals. She paused, sensing the transition before the monitors confirmed it. Then, without a word, she brought over a second chair and sat across from me at the bedside. She remained there, quiet and unhurried. "It won't be long," she said with quiet certainty.

We sat together in the dim illumination. Two people from different worlds, witnessing. She did not summon doctors or adjust the IV.

She simply remained and with her presence, honored what was happening. It was the most important instance of shared presence. It established a tacit agreement to allow this passage its natural unfolding.

When the monitors finally registered what we already knew, she muted the alarms before they could sound. She checked her watch and noted the time. Her movements were precise and professional yet infused with a reverence for the significance of the passage.

"I'll give you some time," she said, and left the room.

I sat with my friend's body until the first light appeared. It illuminated the wooden bowl. I stood, straightened his blanket, and bowed in farewell.

Later, a young monk at the temple asked what I had learned at the hospital. He anticipated stories of institutional coldness. Battling medical bureaucracy. Standing fixed against technological intrusion into the transition.

I told him about the nurse who brought a cushion. About the resident who measured his steps. About the night nurse who sat and witnessed without intervention. About the doctor who recognized the limits of medical questions.

"I did not change the hospital," I explained. "Nor did it change me. But in the space between our worlds, there were intervals of mutual recognition that required neither conversion nor compromise."

Beside the *bochi*, the small cemetery on temple grounds, the cherry trees are blooming today. Their petals fall on the stone marker, on the moss. The morning light continues to illuminate the wooden bowl, now returned to its shelf in the temple kitchen. The petals do not fall with intention or purpose. They are released from the tree when their time comes, their descent neither hurried nor delayed.

The most effective approach to resolving conflict contains neither argument nor persuasion. It is the practice of authentic presence. Being fully who you are in places designed for other purposes. Not to convert or confront, but to complement. Sometimes, through the serene demonstration of an alternative possibility made visible, this changes everything.

The Broken Gate
When Being Right Is Not the Whole Truth

The morning air has the cool, crisp edge of autumn touched with the faint scent of pine. Along the eastern path, the stone lantern casts its angled shadow across our feet. From here, you can see the outer gate of the temple grounds. Weathered by time, the wood no longer demands notice yet holds the eye all the same. It stands in that balance where form and landscape meet, unforced, unhidden.

A temple is not only walls and wood. It is also made of gestures: the way one bows before entering, the way silence is carried from one room to another. These small, unspoken acts are the true beams of the practice.

Still, wood matters. A threshold must be built before it can be crossed.

That outer gate had stood for more than a century. Hands had polished the grain smooth. Weather had darkened its tones. A junior monk once called it "our second bow," because even the uninitiated seemed to pause there.

In summer, it groaned when opened, low and musical. In winter, the cold gave it a higher voice. I had come to know its seasons by sound.

One late autumn afternoon, a delivery truck arrived with timber for a repair project. The driver was young, unfamiliar. His movements had the hurried tension of someone behind schedule. Despite careful instructions, he backed too close to the stone path and caught the side of the gate's support post with the rear of his vehicle.

The sound it made was not loud. But it was wrong. A kind of reluctant tearing, followed by a dead quiet more final than any noise.

I arrived seconds later. The post had moved, only by a few centimeters, but enough. A vertical that had run from earth to sky was no longer straight.

The driver bowed deeply with formal words of apology. His voice was gruff, his face flushed. Then, as I signed the delivery form, he hesitated. Glancing again at the gate, he murmured that perhaps it had already been like that. That he wasn't sure.

No one corrected him. But the air around us had changed.

The junior monk said almost in a whisper, "He knew."

Another, older monk said the company should be held responsible. Not in anger, just with the certainty that this was how things are made right.

I said nothing. The light had begun to stretch. Shadows ran long. The gate looked back at us with its new aspect, as if it had absorbed the alteration with a calm dignity.

That night, the matter returned over the meal. Some spoke of justice, others of accountability. A few said we should repair it ourselves, as we had always done. Each view made sense. Each, in its own way, was complete.

After evening meditation, I returned to the gate. The full moon had risen. The cracked post caught the light differently now, as if it no longer blended into the whole, but declared itself.

I crouched and touched the wood. It had not splintered. It had moved.

The next morning, I returned with tools: a wrapped mallet, wedge stones, a brace. I worked slowly. Not restoring what had been but listening for what could be. I eased the post toward balance. Not perfect, but stable. The gate began to move again. Its voice was changed. But it opened.

Later, the junior monk came to ask why I had done the repair myself. He asked whether we should have pursued accountability. Whether letting it go was weakness.

I told him: The driver had made one error in striking the gate, and another in trying to modify the story. That second one was harder to witness. Truth matters.

But so does wholeness. If we had pressed forward with calls and blame, we may have restored the wood. But perhaps we would have cracked a part of the relationship that was not visible, not easily repaired. He asked whether this meant absorbing the harm.

"No," I said. "It means seeing the full field. It means choosing not what is correct, but what is complete."

We sat in the morning light. A few sparrows moved through the gravel, pausing between each burst of flight.

I said, "He did not act from cruelty. Perhaps it was fear. Perhaps his job is fragile. Perhaps he could not admit fault without unraveling a thread within. One crack can lead to another."

"We repair what we can reach," the monk said. "The gate. Not the man."

"Exactly," I replied. "And yet, perhaps a part of him will remember."

That week, the senior monk who had first spoken of justice approached me after zazen. He said he had come to see his reaction differently. That it wasn't really about repair. It was about reassurance.

"Reassurance of what?" I asked.

"That the world works according to my sense of fairness."

You will encounter many broken gates in this life. Occasions when you are right. When another has erred. When the path to correction is clear and available.

At those times, pause. Ask not only what will fix the damage, but what will preserve the whole. What will honor the human, not just the rule. What will leave you not only justified, but unbroken.

Not all fractures are meant to be forced closed. Some must be met with patience. With hands that listen.

The gate continues to stand. Its shape is altered. Its sound is new. Its shadow bends slightly further in the late day sun. But it opens. It holds. It receives.

And each time I pass through it, I remember: Some things, once altered, are not meant to be restored. They are meant to be received.

The Space Between Sentences
Hearing the Deeper Meaning

He did not bow when he entered. That was the first sign. He closed the sliding door firmly, almost forcefully, and stood for an instant, deciding whether to sit. When he finally did, it was not the way one settles in to speak with calm. It was the bearing of someone ready to make his case.

"You speak often of presence," he began. "But I don't think you actually practice it."

I waited.

"You've told me to bring my whole self," he continued. "To stop hiding. But every time I show you what is real for me, my anger and doubt, you sit there as though I have said nothing at all. Or you reply with a quiet word like 'Ah' or 'I see,' and then you change the subject. Or worse, you turn it into a lesson."

I nodded not because he was right or wrong, but because I heard him.

"I came here," he said, "because I didn't want therapy. I didn't want fixing. I wanted to learn how to face things directly. But now I wonder if you even see me. Or if I'm just a mirror you use to say the same things again and again."

His voice wasn't raised, but it was tight. He was holding back a force within himself. "You're angry," I said.

"Yes."

"You feel dismissed."

"Yes."

"You want to be seen, not studied."

"Yes."

I let those words rest. Not because they were new, but because they had never been given space before.

After a while, I asked, "When did that feeling begin?"

He looked confused. "What feeling?"

"The feeling that presence is a gift others are allowed to receive, but not you."

He looked at me, eyes narrowing. "What are you trying to say?"

"I'm asking when that story began."

He leaned back. "You think this is about my childhood."

"No," I said. "I think it's about this room. Right now. But it's a long story. And I don't think I'm the first person you've had to test."

He stared at the floor. "I'm not trying to test you."

"You are," I said. "And that's not a failure. That's a longing."

He didn't respond.

I continued, slowly. "There is a part of you that is not convinced anyone can stay with you when you're angry. When you're hurt, when you're raw, you push, just a little, to see if I'll go away. Or retreat behind a wise saying. Or offer silence you can interpret as withdrawal."

He looked up. His face was no longer angry. Only tired.

"I thought presence meant offering myself," he said.

"It does."

"But I did. And I felt alone."

"You offered your anger," I said. "But underneath that, you were waiting for rejection. You were watching for it. And when it didn't come, you felt emptier, not fuller."

"I didn't want to admit that."

"I know."

We sat without speaking for several minutes. His body loosened. The lines in his forehead changed.

Then he asked, "Why didn't you respond earlier? All those times I said things that were barbed or critical. Why didn't you say anything?"

"Because I wasn't interested in reacting," I said. "I was listening."

"To what?"

"To what hadn't yet been said."

He breathed out slowly.

"I wanted to matter to you," he said.

"You do."

"I wanted to hear it."

"You are hearing it now."

He shook his head. "But I didn't want to *ask* for it. I wanted it to come uninvited."

"Of course you did," I said. "Because if it comes uninvited, you don't have to fear that it was given out of pity. Or politeness. Or obligation."

He closed his eyes. "Yes."

We let the quiet return. It was different now. Not a silence of pressure or avoidance. But of breath. Of settling.

After a while, I added, "I did see your anger. But I didn't want to answer your fire with fire. I didn't want to defend or instruct. I wanted to stay."

He opened his eyes. "And you think that was enough?"

"It wasn't what you wanted. But it may have been what you needed."

He looked down. "I think I expected you to fail me."

"I know."

He looked back at me. "You're not going to."

"Not today."

He laughed quietly. "That's honest."

"I can't promise I will always meet you perfectly," I said. "But I can promise that I will meet you. Not your performance. Not your social mask. You."

He let out a long breath and leaned back slightly. Not relaxed, but less guarded.

"This has been the hardest part," he said.

"What part?"

"Not being answered."

"But you were answered," I said. "Just not in the language of argument. Or reassurance."

"I'm not trying to win," he said. "I just… I didn't want to disappear."

"You haven't," I said. "You're here. Fully."

Presence in conflict is not a pause before reply. It is the refusal to defend when accused. The refusal to fix when confronted. The refusal to retreat when someone burns too brightly with pain. Presence listens without preparing to speak. And when it speaks, it responds to what is true, not just what is loud.

There will always be those occasions when someone needs you to absorb their heat without flinching. To remain calm when their voice shakes. To see the wound behind the anger and answer that directly. This is not silence. It is love with its armor removed.

PART IV

Integration and Wisdom

Transformation and Embodied Presence

The Brush That Paints Nothing
The Space Between Words

In the room behind the *zendo*, the meditation hall, Yamada Roshi prepared for calligraphy. As a young monk, I watched as he slowly ground the ink stone, adding water drop by drop. He arranged the washi paper, its four corners positioned precisely with the edges of the table. Then, lifting his arm, he held the brush above the white surface of the paper. His hand and arm remained suspended, like a gesture incomplete and frozen in time. Then he lowered the brush without making a mark.

Once, after watching in silence, I could not contain my curiosity.

"Why did you not paint anything?"

He smiled. "Why do you assume that there is nothing?"

I looked at the untouched paper, uncertain.

"Look," he said, gesturing toward the rock garden visible through the open door, "What do you see?"

I saw raked gravel among precisely placed stones.

"There are stones and spaces between the stones," I replied.

"And which speaks more clearly?" he asked.

"Both are important," I said. "Without the stones there would be no garden. Without the space between the stones there would also be no garden."

"The stones are what the designer placed and their positioning establishes the spaces among them. Perhaps you could say that the stones are the garden. Or you could say the spaces around the stones are the garden. Both are true. What is set down and what is left unfilled carry equal presence."

We returned to the table with its untouched paper. He lifted the brush and, with fluid strokes, drew a single character.

間

"Here is *ma*, the space between," he said. "*Ma* is not emptiness. It is the active silence that allows form to breathe, meaning to emerge, and relationship to unfold."

The character was clear and strong, but it was the surrounding space that gave it breath.

"In our conversations," he continued, "what we do not say creates the *ma*, the space around our words."

Some weeks later, I saw the truth of his teaching during a tense meeting between the *fusu*, the temple treasurer, and the *enzu*, the monk who managed the vegetable garden.

For three years, the chief garden monk had argued that funds were urgently needed for a new irrigation system. Each time the garden monk made his request, the treasurer listened patiently and then cited limited resources and pressing priorities. Their repetitive conversations had grown tense, each speaking past the other, each becoming ever more entrenched in his position.

This particular conversation began in the usual way. The garden monk spoke urgently about wasted water, long hours, and the promise of better yields. The treasurer listened, already forming his response before the other had finished.

Then the rhythm broke.

After the garden monk concluded, the treasurer began to speak but paused. He closed his eyes for a heartbeat. When he opened them again, he remained quiet.

In that silence, an easing occurred. The bearing and energy of both men softened. The edge of argument faded, giving way to a quieter, more open exchange.

When the treasurer finally spoke, his words were fewer and clearer than before. He acknowledged the need. He explained the constraints and did not repeat the usual objections.

Most importantly, he left unspoken the comments that would have added only heat: the complaint about too many requests, the quiet resentment of being misunderstood. What remained unsaid created the space in which understanding could begin to grow. They did not reach a resolution. But for the first time, they heard each other.

Later, I asked the treasurer what had prompted his restraint.

"I realized I was filling every space with words," he said. "No wonder the garden monk couldn't hear me. There was no room for my meaning to breathe."

He paused. "Strangely, by saying less, I think I finally said what mattered."

We often assume that more words create more clarity. We fear that silence will consume our message. The wisdom of *ma*, emptiness, tells us otherwise. Without space there is no breath. There is no room to hear.

In your next conversation, especially one filled with heat or misunderstanding, notice the impulse to speak. Then wait. Let your words rest. Be like the calligrapher who understands the expressiveness of the space around the line.

Ask yourself: What is important for me not to say? Which words, if left unspoken, could create space for understanding? Which explanations or grievances may crowd this fleeting instance?

Not every brushstroke serves the form. The most meaningful communication, like the most expressive calligraphy, knows when the brush should touch the paper and when it should remain lifted.

The words we choose not to speak form the *ma* of each conversation. The space between is what allows understanding to take root.

Sometimes, the brush that paints nothing leaves the deepest impression of all.

Moment of Totality

A Glimpse of Oneness

I had been at the monastery for six years when the letter arrived folded in thirds. It had been mailed from my family's village. The writing was unmistakable. Obaachan's hand, steady but slowing.

"Come if you can," it read. "The garden is asking for you."

I brought the letter to the abbot the next morning. He read it once, then placed it on the windowsill and looked out toward the sea.

"Your grandmother was the one who raised you?" he asked.

"Yes, Roshi."

He returned the letter to me with a smile. That was permission. I departed a few hours later.

On the flight to Sapporo no one spoke to the young, black-robed monk in the window seat. From the air, Hokkaido appeared dark green against a blue sea, bordered by the rocky coast.

I took the Airport train from Chitose to Otaru where I boarded a bus to Shakotan. I sat quietly beside a middle-aged man reading a newspaper. He handed me a hard-boiled egg without speaking.

The bus travelled west past rice fields and coastal villages. I exited at a familiar place on the road marked by a weathered sign that was no longer legible. I walked the final mile through cedar groves until I arrived in the village where my family took their livelihoods from the sea.

Like most fishing villages in Hokkaido at that time, it was a small community living in a cluster of one-story wooden buildings between sea and mountains. At dawn, fishermen would congregate at the harbor, check their nets and discuss weather conditions before going out to sea.

The house was as I remembered it: the stone wall built and maintained by Ojiichan; the single pine leaning over the eaves; the red maple in full leaf. Obaachan's garden surrounded the house. Squash vines covered the wall. Plum trees leaned away from the ocean breeze. Rain-shaped stones edged a bed of mugwort.

Obaachan opened the door before I knocked. She bowed, then stepped aside.

We spoke little. She handed me a bowl of hot miso soup and a small dish of pickled radish. Ojiichan appeared later, his sleeves rolled and eyes clear and alert despite his years. He looked at my shaved head, grunted, and asked if I had learned anything yet. I said I was continuing to practice.

That evening, as we sat around the low table after dinner, Obaachan's questions began with care.

"Do you miss Ojiichan's sake?" she asked, watching me eat the fish and vegetables she had prepared.

"I remember it," I said. "But I don't long for it."

"And New Year with family?"

I felt the weight behind her question. "I remember."

"Yet, you abandoned us."

Ojiichan sighed. "How many years?" he said.

The three words were more accusation than question.

Outside, the wind moved softly through the maple branches.

"But it wasn't enough for you."

"It wasn't about enough," I said.

"What did you find in those mountains that you couldn't find here?"

I looked at Ojiichan's weathered palms, the same hands that had taught me to tie fishing knots, to recognize the signs of changing weather. How could I explain the certainty that had led me away from everything familiar?

"I found tranquility," I said. "But perhaps I lost part of myself."

Ojiichan's expression softened slightly. "You lost us. For a while."

"Will you watch the eclipse with us?" Obaachan asked as she prepared tea.

I heard the invitation beneath her words. It was not just to witness the eclipse but to take part in what the village would experience together.

"Yes," I said.

That night, the village did not sleep. We walked to the harbor just after midnight. The pier had been cleared. Paper lanterns swayed in the wind. Small teams had arrived earlier that day: astronomers, physicists, and atmospheric experts. They arranged their telescopes, cameras, spectrographs, and photometers on the western bluff with focused urgency.

Children whispered in fascination. The energy in the air was taut like the final inhalation before a storm.

By 2:30 AM, people began to gather. Some carried rice balls, others thermoses. There were no cars. Only the sound of soft sandals and the sea.

We walked the old path along the ridge. At its crest, the land opened westward into a high, grassy bluff where sea met sky. We found places near the edge. Obaachan sat on a small folding stool Ojiichan had brought. I sat cross-legged on the ground beside her.

Around us, the village had assembled.

Kano, a fisherman I had once known, sat nearby, smoking a cigarette. He recognized me. "Back from the mountain?" he asked.

"For a visit."

He looked up at the luminous stars. "The sun will rise and then the sky will go dark."

I smiled, remembering our conversations of long ago. "But not like night. Just a different kind of shadow."

Knowledge of the rare solar event extended far beyond the isolated, rugged shores of my grandparents' home. The village had spent years preparing for this occasion. The village, once known only to those who sought *bafun uni*, a rare premium seafood delicacy, now appeared on international maps.

Scientists came from Australia, Europe, America and even the Soviet Union. They brought delicate equipment to record the corona's composition. They had made the long and difficult journey to this remote place only for a few minutes of totality.

Local government officials established safe viewing points and media from many countries sent camera crews. Every room in the village's few inns had been reserved years in advance. A great many visitors stayed in

Sapporo, the capital city, 100 miles away. They would spend much of the night travelling to the village. The eclipse would begin at dawn.

By 3:00 AM, thousands had assembled at the official observation locations. The mood combined the formal focus of a scientific experiment, the reverence of a spiritual ritual, and a carnival atmosphere. There was a light sea breeze, clear and cool. Perfect viewing conditions.

Obaachan reached over and touched my arm. "I used to wonder if you thought about us when you sat in meditation."

"I thought of you every day," I said.

"But you never came back."

"I thought my leaving had to mark a lasting break."

"And now?"

"Now I think maybe I was afraid you'd ask me to explain what couldn't be explained."

At 3:52 AM, the eclipse began.

I stood between two worlds. On one side were teams of scientists engrossed in their optical and radio equipment. They conversed in terse, technical phrases, their attention directed at their instruments.

On my other side, stood villagers. These were fishermen whose weather-lined faces had witnessed countless dawns over these waters, elderly couples who had moved through decades together, children experiencing their first eclipse. They carried the simple smoked glass viewers that had been distributed throughout the village. Their conversations were experiential, filled with impressions, memories, and sensations. Their attention was direct. The naked eye encountering natural phenomena with minimal mediation.

As the moon took its first small bite from the sun's edge, the contrast between the two groups became more pronounced. The scientists spoke of timestamps while they used technology with methodical precision. The villagers pointed, exclaimed, and shared their immediate impressions of the changing luminosity and temperature, the unusual behavior of birds that began to settle as if for evening.

There were two distinct modes of attention, one investigative, the other experiential. They seemed to represent distinct realities occupied by people standing only meters apart.

In the final seconds before totality, a transfiguration occurred. The illumination took on an unearthly quality. It was not the warm glow of sunset but a light unfamiliar, almost otherworldly. Shadows sharpened to remarkable clarity. The temperature dropped as hush fell over the coastline.

Then totality arrived.

The sun's disk disappeared behind the moon, revealing the corona, a silver halo of plasma. Stars appeared in the mid-morning sky. The horizon glowed in all directions with the colors of sunset, as if the sun were simultaneously setting everywhere and nowhere.

In the blackness of this rare night superimposed on the dawn of a new day, an event beyond expectation unfolded. The scientists looked up from their instruments. The villagers lowered their pieces of smoked glass. For the one-hundred seconds of totality, scientific documentation and direct experience converged. Two modes of perception had become one shared reality that transcended all frameworks.

No one spoke. There was only awareness. Only attention. A single, shared gaze upon a phenomenon that touched all equally, revealing a truth beyond both analysis and intuition.

When the first beam of sunlight broke from behind the moon, it elicited a collective response that transcended professional and cultural boundaries. Some gasped. Others remained in speechless awe. All stood motionless, as if reluctant to break an enchanted whisper in time by returning to ordinary movement and speech.

As daylight returned, the distinct approaches resumed. Scientists focused on their instruments, completing their work. Villagers shared their emotional responses. Yet a change had occurred in the quality of their separation. Boundaries remained but had become more permeable.

"It's beautiful," Obaachan whispered.

"Yes," I said.

"Is this what you found? This kind of beauty?"

I turned to look at her. In the strange, silvering radiance, her face held the same wonder as the children around us.

"This is what I was looking for," I said. "But I think I could have found it here too."

Ojiichan, who hadn't touched me since I was a child, placed his palm on my shoulder.

There was no separation between the monk who had left and the grandson who had returned. No difference between the seeker and the sought. Only this instant, shared, complete.

Ojiichan removed his palm from my shoulder.

"Thank you," Obaachan said. "For returning and sharing this with us."

We walked together to the harbor in the early morning radiance. The village was hushed but it felt like a different kind of tranquility. Not the quiet of turning away, but the calm of seeing clearly.

"The eclipse won't happen here again until the year 2200," Ojiichan said.

"Maybe not," I agreed.

I stayed three more days. We spoke little about my life at the monastery or their years without me. But a quiet connection had been restored, one that didn't depend on words.

When I left, Obaachan walked with me to the gate.

"You don't have to explain your life to us," she said. "We just want to know that you hadn't erased us from your heart."

"Never," I said.

There are turning points when the distance between the life we chose and the life we left behind softens into shared understanding. In the darkness of totality, I was the monk and the grandson, the seeker and the one who never left a small village by the sea.

Resolution is not always found by solving what divides us, but by standing together in the presence of a truth larger than any single story.

36

One-Time One-Meeting

The Uniqueness of Each Moment

The koi have been swimming in the garden pond for centuries. Their motion through the water etches shapes that disappear even as they form. Consider the *kumonryu*, black and white. Their colors change over time. Sometimes almost all white, sometimes dark as ink. Does any pattern of motion remain carved in the water? The water accepts each new shape without hesitation.

The bright orange koi swims beneath the lily pad, while a pale one turns. This fleeting instant of time, this second of movement, this light and shadow, will never happen again. This is *ichi-go ichi-e*. One time one meeting.

The tea master prepares bowls of tea with full presence. Every guest, every gesture, every silence holds the burden of finality. The master knows: this gathering, these people, this hour, will never occur again in this exact way.

Incense smoke rises in the *zendo*, the meditation hall, in a column, curves and disappears. Look away for an instant and you miss that shape forever. The same is true when we speak with another person. A conversation may look like one we have had before. But it is not. The face before you, the tone, the fears, the hesitations, the emotions, none of it is the same. And neither are you.

But we forget. We bring our memory of the last encounter, our expectations of what should happen, our ideas about who this person is. And in doing so, we miss what is actually before us. We rehearse answers to questions not yet asked. We prepare for battles that may never come.

As a child, I watched Ojiichan, my grandfather, sit with a neighbor arguing about land both believed was theirs. They argued intensely. Then, the tone changed. Ojiichan set down his teacup and said, "Tell me, right now, what matters most to you about this piece of earth?"

It was not a clever question. It was a present one. And it was a turning point. In that instant, they both returned to what was real.

When you look at a person and see him not as a role or a memory, but as who he is now, your attention becomes a form of respect. You are not managing him. You are not defending yourself. You are here.

Even when disagreement arises, this way of seeing matters. Conflict, too, is unrepeatable. The resistance you meet today is different from yesterday. If you meet it with fresh eyes, you may hear a truth in the tension that would otherwise remain buried.

Words once spoken cannot be withdrawn. Like brushstrokes in ink, they carry your state of mind into the world. Were you hurried? Were you clear? Were you listening? Each word leaves its trace. Not in permanence, but in effect.

When a meeting ends, let it end. Do not carry it forward as a burden. Do not replay the words. Let it be like the koi's movement across the pond. No record remains. Only the echo of presence.

Each time you face another person, remember: this meeting is not a rehearsal. You have never seen him quite like this before. You will not again. See clearly. Speak from the calm beneath your knowing.

The Path of Jizō

On Walking With the Struggling Other

There is a row of weathered statues behind the main hall, tucked between pine trees and moss-covered stones. Each one is Jizō. Some wear hand-knitted caps. Others have red bibs, faded and frayed. A few have small pebbles placed at their feet, or tiny wind chimes hanging from nearby branches. They are offerings, acts of devotion left by parents, grandparents, those grieving or afraid.

Jizō does not carry anyone. He does not remove the stones from the path. He simply stands. Sometimes he walks. His power lies not in what he changes, but in how he remains.

There was once a woman who spoke to me about her younger sister. "She resists every kindness," she said. "When I try to help, she says I'm controlling. When I step back, she says I don't care. I feel like I can't win."

I listened.

"You are trying to lead her up the mountain," I said. "But have you ever walked beside her?"

She looked uncertain. "If I don't guide her, she'll stay stuck."

"Perhaps," I said. "Or perhaps she will find her own footing if someone is near enough to keep her from despair, but not so close that she cannot take a single step alone."

She said nothing for a while. Then she asked, "What if she never moves?"

"Then you will have accompanied her in her motionlessness."

Conflict often arises not because one person is wrong, but because the pace between two people has diverged. One moves quickly, fueled by clarity or urgency. The other slows, tangled by doubt or fear. The difference becomes friction. Words sharpen. Silence thickens.

But presence does not mean rushing to fix. Nor does it mean withdrawal. It means remaining. Attuned.

If the other person stumbles for words, let your quiet be a vessel rather than a void. That silence can become a clearing, a space in which her voice may find itself again.

And when she pushes back, seemingly without cause, ask gently: Is this resistance? Or is it a signal that I am walking too far ahead?

The mountain path is not only for the swift. The view at the summit does not fade because it takes longer to reach. The slower journey reveals more: a twisted root hidden beneath leaves, the scent of earth after rain, the quiet companionship of a bird tracing the same path.

Strength in conflict does not originate from dominance. It rises from the capacity to remain present without coercion. To be rooted without hardening. To offer dignity when dignity is not being offered in return.

The bamboo bends in the wind and returns upright. So also, can people if they are allowed to bend without being broken.

When conflict arises, remember Jizō. Hands folded. Face worn smooth. Not absent. Not indifferent. Present. Witnessing. Waiting. Walking in step.

You do not need to carry the other person. But you can walk beside her, long enough for her own strength to return.

38

The Mountain and the Lotus

Returning After Doubt

There was a time I considered leaving the path. It was early in my training during the late summer. The routines felt endless. I had begun to memorize chants without hearing them. My meditation form was precise, but my heart had become silent in a way that did not bring calm.

I told no one. Not even my teacher. I carried it in silence, like a fault line beneath a temple floor.

One morning, after a rain storm, I was sent to deliver a scroll to a temple in the foothills. The task was simple. I chose to take a different route back. I told myself the forest path would be quicker. It was not.

I walked for hours. The trail narrowed. The incline steepened. Eventually the path disappeared. I found myself on a low ridge, facing a slope of loose stone. Behind me was the way I had come. Ahead, the mountain descended into mist.

I stood there, unsure. The scroll had been delivered. No one would ask why I arrived late. I considered never returning. Not out of defiance. Out of weariness. It was not the form I doubted, or the teachings. I doubted myself.

I began to descend the slope.

The stones gave way beneath my feet. I fell once. Then again. My robe tore along one side. My hand bled where it caught a jagged edge.

By the time I reached the base, I was covered in dust and silent anger.

I walked until I found water. A shallow pond surrounded by reeds. The wind moved across it, barely. Near the center, one lotus stood.

It was not blooming. The flower was closed, tilted slightly. But it had risen through mud and water to reach the light.

I sat beside the pond and waited.

There was no sudden instance of awareness. Only the sense that a quiet presence had witnessed my descent and remained.

I stayed until the light changed.

Then I stood and turned toward the monastery.

When I arrived, the gates were closed for evening meditation. I bowed before entering, my robe torn and spotted with mud.

No one spoke.

The *jikijitsu* looked at me without expression as I took my seat.

I have never told anyone where I went that day. But I return there often in memory.

Sometimes the conflict we carry is not with others. It is not loud. It does not name itself. It waits beneath the surface. And when that happens, presence is not heroic. It is not clarity or confidence. It is the simple act of staying through the doubt.

When you question the path, know that this too is part of it. Not a detour. Not a failure.

Let the question rise.

Let your feet slip.

Let your robe tear.

Then, when you are ready, sit beside the pond.

The lotus does not bloom because it is unbroken. It blooms because it returns.

39

The Drift

On What Does Not Move

The ferry had just pulled away from the dock. The wind had picked up. Cold air moved easily over the open water, slapping lightly against the rails. We were only fifteen minutes into the crossing when the engine stopped.

There was no loud sound. Just a gradual change. The low, constant vibration beneath our feet faded. A second passed. Then another.

People looked around. A crew member appeared, then disappeared below deck.

The announcement came over the speaker a few minutes later.

"We're experiencing a power issue. We're working to restart the engine. Please stay calm. The ferry is adrift. We will update you shortly."

That was all.

I was standing near the stern, outside on the lower deck. It was not crowded. A few passengers beside me moved away to look for more information. One remained. A man around forty, in a dark blue coat. His hands were on the rail.

Slowly, without force, the ferry began to turn. A slight angle of drift in the breeze. The city came into view. Then the pier. Then, gradually, the sound of wind pressing into the side of the ship.

The man beside me exhaled, short and tight.

"I don't like this," he said.

I said nothing.

He added, "I don't panic. But I don't like not knowing."

The pier grew larger, closer.

"Will we hit it?" he asked.

"I don't know," I said.

He was silent for a while.

Others had come to the windows. Some were holding their phones, filming. A child near the upper deck was crying, but quietly.

He said, "You seem calm."

I looked out at the pier.

He glanced over. "Aren't you afraid?"

"Not yet," I said.

"Why not?"

"I think I'm still here," I said.

He frowned slightly. "What does that mean?"

I didn't answer immediately. The ferry turned slightly.

I said, "Fear is real. But sometimes we reach for it before it arrives. Sometimes we think about what may happen, and our bodies begin to live there before anything unfolds."

The pier loomed larger now. We could see the lines of the dock. The thick wood, wet and black at the waterline. The drifting continued at the same speed.

He said, "So you are unconcerned?"

His voice was tight with tension, trying to find a place to grip.

I shook my head. "No. I'm standing here."

He gave a short laugh. "What's the point of just watching?"

I turned toward him slightly.

"I'm not saying it changes the situation," I said. "But it keeps me from being taken by it."

He said nothing.

I added, "There's a part of you that can feel the fear and not become it. That part is here now, even while we drift."

He looked out toward the pier again.

The ferry's speaker came on once more.

"We're working to restart the engine. Please remain calm. A tugboat is on its way. Estimated arrival, ten minutes."

The man exhaled.

"Ten minutes," he said. "That's enough time to imagine every possible outcome."

Then, without turning, he said, "You don't seem worried."

I said nothing at first. Then, "Not yet."

He gave a small exhale. "I don't mean to overreact. I don't like not knowing what's going on."

The wind changed direction again. The ferry turned a little more.

After a pause, he said, "How are you staying so calm?"

"There's a part of us," I said, "that watches, unmoved, as time flows. It's not stirred by fear, and it doesn't settle with relief. It's just here. Now."

He glanced at me, then back at the water. "Is that a truth you learned through your meditation practice?"

"In part," I said. "But also, by noticing. This part isn't created, it doesn't come and go. It just doesn't drift."

He was silent again, but his posture changed. Not comfort, but recognition.

A change in wind direction carried us in a new direction. We were no longer drifting toward the pier.

He saw it too.

"We might miss it," he said.

"We might," I said.

The tension in his face did not vanish, but his features had softened. Not relief. But recognition.

We stood there without speaking as the ferry turned slightly again. The tugboat became visible behind us.

We didn't hit the pier.

It passed at a safe distance, slow and massive. People clapped in scattered relief. The engines did not return, but the ferry's motion had stopped. The tugboat would guide us in.

He exhaled once more.

"I don't know why, but I feel calmer now than I did ten minutes ago."

"I think you were here for it," I said.

He gave a slight nod. Then he left the rail and went inside.

I remained a while longer.

Not every danger arrives with sound and force. Some drift toward us slowly, silently, offering just enough time to imagine what might happen. And sometimes that imagining is what unsettles us the most.

Presence is not calmness. It is not courage. It is not what keeps the ship from striking the pier. It is what moves without collision. It is what watches. And stays. Even as the wind pushes. Even as the hull turns. Even as you wait, not knowing.

Steps Along the Cliff
Presence Amid What Cannot Be Resolved

It was a gray afternoon, late in the season when the leaves fall with the wind. I was walking along a narrow coastal path along the cliff edge. Below, quiet waves lapped against the shore. Here there was the sky and the sea, and a trail worn by the steps of all those who had walked here before.

I had stopped in the village to buy a small package of dried persimmons. It had been many years since I had traveled through that region. Once, long ago, I had spent two weeks there in solitude.

Along the path, I came upon a man and a woman standing apart from one another. They were not speaking, though their faces bore the tension of recent words. Their postures were careful. Each stood as if waiting for the other to decide whether the conversation would resume or end. Neither looked at the sea. Their eyes remained fixed on the ground.

Just as I came near, the woman turned slightly toward the man and said, "You never see what matters to me. You only hear what you think I should want."

The man replied with neither harshness nor heat. "I don't know what you want anymore. I don't think you do either."

Then silence. Not resolved. Not broken. Just held.

I continued walking, but the quiet they had left behind walked with me.

There is a kind of silence that feels like breath held just before speech. The air between them carried that quality. Not final. But taut with the possibility of further harm. Or healing.

We speak of presence, but presence is not simply being in the same place or hearing the same words. It is meeting the moment with no residue of expectation, no claim of knowing, no leaning forward into a conclusion. It is letting each word arrive as if for the first time, without folding it into a story already unfolding in the mind.

The woman had spoken with hurt, but also clarity. The man had replied with weariness, but not cruelty. What neither could offer was the space between. Unfilled, unforced, undesigned.

Many conflicts arise not from the words spoken but from the weight of what those words are made to carry. A question becomes an accusation. A hesitation becomes a betrayal. We do not meet what is said. We meet what we believe has already been said too many times before.

Presence does not erase pain. It does not prevent misunderstanding. But it slows the movement of mind long enough for the shape of the other to emerge. Not the version constructed by our fear or history, but the person before us, breathing in this moment, saying only what she is saying.

Further down the path, I found a flat stone and sat for a time. The sea below moved in long, steady waves. No drama. Just the rhythm of water against earth.

I remembered a time, many years earlier, when I had spoken too quickly in a conversation that mattered. A dear friend had opened up, cautiously. I replied too quickly, too sure of myself. He fell silent. The ease between us faded. Later, I realized it was not my words that had caused the break, but my lack of presence. I had not met him where he was. I had met my idea of him. I had spoken to that idea and not to the man in front of me.

Presence would not have required me to say more. Only less. Only what was truly responsive to that moment, and nothing more.

The couple I passed that day remained behind me, both on the trail and in time. I do not know whether they reconciled or parted. But I remember the space between their words. I remember how it held a question that neither had yet answered.

That question lives in many conversations. It asks, "Can you meet me without your history of me?" It asks, "Can you receive my words without projecting meaning that isn't there?" It asks, "Can you be here, not with your defenses, but with your breath?"

When the next conversation grows difficult, attend to what is actually being said. Let go of the thread of old conclusions. Do not reach backward or forward. Remain quiet. Listen not only for meaning, but for the moment itself. Hear the voice before you like a bell you have never heard before.

Do not interrupt with understanding.

Let the other arrive.

Let yourself arrive.

We are always more than the stories we have already told.

41

The Sword That Gives Life
The Power of Clear Words

In the martial arts schools influenced by Zen, there is a precise distinction: *satsujinken*, the "sword that kills," and *katsujinken*, the "sword that gives life." The contrast is not about violence. It is a message about discernment and presence.

Satsujinken, the sword that kills, cuts away delusion. Wrong ideas resulting from pride or fear. It is the harsh word spoken in anger, the truth used as a weapon, the desire to win rather than understand. It leads to argument and leaves damage in its wake.

Katsujinken, the sword that gives life, cuts through turmoil without cutting the person. It is confrontational without being aggressive. Honest, but not punishing. By revealing rather than wounding, it awakens.

I once saw this principle in the words of a lay practitioner, named Himari. She had practiced with us for many years. One morning, I passed her speaking with her younger sister beneath the gingko tree. Their conversation was subdued, but I felt its heaviness.

Later, Himari shared what had passed between them. "My sister has been hurting," she said. "But she lashes out. For a long time, I tried to be gentle. I avoided saying what needed to be said. I thought that was kindness. But it only allowed the pattern to continue. This morning, I said to my sister, 'I love you, but you should understand that your anger is harmful. It is driving people away. Including me.' My sister cried but did not walk away. She heard me," Himari said. "Heard me for the first time in many years."

That is the sword that gives life.

In swordsmanship, both *satsujinken* and *katsujinken* are born of the same instrument. But the mind behind the stroke determines the outcome. A strike from ego divides. A strike from compassion liberates. The outer action may look similar. The inner source makes all the difference.

So, it is with words.

Many of us have been taught to hold back, to avoid confrontation, to maintain calm through silence or vague language. And sometimes, that is diplomatic. But when clarity is needed and avoided, relationships become unstable. What is unspoken thickens the air. Presence becomes obscured.

Wu-wei, the Taoist principle of effortless action, teaches that the right movement often comes when we stop interfering. But sometimes the most effortless action is a clean truth, spoken from quietness.

There is a difference between saying, "You are impossible," and saying, "I feel pushed away when we speak like this, and I miss our connection."

The first strikes to wound. The second opens a door.

The sword that gives life may be painful. It may cause someone to pause, to question, to feel. But it does not sever the relationship. It reveals the place where honesty can begin.

Silence, too, can become *satsujinken* if it is used to punish. When presence is replaced by withdrawal, even quiet can cause harm. But when silence is held with care, it can become *katsujinken* in its own form -- a gesture of space, a refusal to escalate, a point in time offered to allow the other to return on his own.

The samurai in previous centuries were taught not only technique, but restraint. The sword was not drawn unless absolutely necessary. And when drawn, it was held with respect, not with pride.

So, it is with clear speech. When preparing to respond in a dispute, consider: What is this speech for? Will it deepen division, or create clarity? Am I responding to protect myself, or to invite a deeper truth into the space between us?

The sword that gives life does not react to adverse circumstances. It acts from presence. It does not seek to defeat. It seeks to reveal. And its blade is not intended to harm, but to free.

Clarity of speech must be embedded in compassion. Let your words cut through confusion, not through connection. Let your tone convey balance, not dominance. Your presence should be the sheath that holds the blade in peace. Speak as one who carries the sword that gives life.

The Echo That Heals

Speaking Without Agenda

A cousin, much younger than me asked to meet outside the monastery. He suggested a nearby park. Although we had not spoken in many years, there was no discord. Only the passage of time and the course of different lives. It is the loss of connection that happens when one person enters a monastery and the other remains in the world.

We sat on a wooden bench under a gingko tree, its leaves yellowing with early autumn.

He greeted me politely, asked if I was cold, if I wanted tea. But behind his questions stirred an unease. A current beneath the surface that did not match his words. I waited.

After a few more minutes of polite talk, he paused and exhaled. "You know," he said, "you never visited when she was sick."

I looked at him.

"My mother," he said. "You knew she was in the hospital for weeks. You wrote a note. A very thoughtful note. But you didn't come."

I said nothing.

"She kept asking if you would visit. Even just once."

I let his words fall between us and remain there. Not just the surface words, but the deeper ones. I did not search for a reply. I listened.

"I'm not angry," he added. "But it was strange to realize that the person I was taught to look up to, who always seemed calm and wise, could disappear when someone needed him."

He stopped and looked away. "I always thought you would know when it mattered."

After a breath, I said, "You're saying that I stayed distant when I was needed. That my silence felt like absence. That your mother hoped for a response from me, and I didn't come."

He looked down, hands clasped. "Yes."

"And that you're not sure if I stayed away because of distance or indifference."

"Exactly."

I let his words enter my mind. I did not sort or defend them. I did not prepare to explain.

"You felt unseen in that instant," I said. "Not by everyone. But by me."

"Yes."

"And that made you question whether all the calm and compassion I tried to live by was truly for others, or merely a robe I wore for myself."

His head dropped a little. "Yes."

I waited. Not because I had no words, but because I wanted his words to breathe fully before mine arrived.

"Thank you," I said.

He looked at me, surprised.

"For saying all of that. For not turning it into sarcasm. Or bitterness. Just truth."

He said nothing.

"I did know she was ill," I continued. "And I did think about coming. Many times. I thought perhaps I would cause a disruption. That my appearance would carry more weight than help. I sent a letter, which I now see was not enough."

He looked up.

"I can't change that now," I said. "But I can say that you were right to speak."

"You don't need to forgive me," I added. "But you deserve to be heard."

He looked at me for a long time. "I just wanted you to listen. Not to reframe the past. Just to hear it."

"You did everything right," I said. "And I remain here."

We sat for a while longer. He asked a few questions about the monastery. I asked about his children. There was no great warmth. No perfect repair. But there was breath again in the space between us.

Presence in conflict is listening with nothing hidden behind the eyes. It is returning someone's words to them, gently, so they know they were heard and understood. It is speaking without desire for any result.

In the Cave of the Blue Dragon
Finding Truth Beyond Words

The branches of the plum trees are knotted with age. Yet, each spring the flowers open without effort. So too, must we open when conversation becomes difficult, when the other's thoughts seem clouded, or their words reach us with the strangeness of another tongue.

There are intervals in any relationship, especially those shaped by conflict, when understanding feels out of reach. You may listen and not hear. You may speak and feel the silence afterward tighten, not relax.

I remember an image from long ago.

In the folds of an ancient mountain range, there is said to be a cave. Hidden, deep, and silent. And within this cave lives a blue dragon. Its body is long and fluid, its scales the color of moonlit water that seems to ripple with unseen motion. The edges of its scales catch light like cut sapphire. Its eyes are deep pools. When it looks at you, it sees through every layer you wear. It knows the place before thought arises.

Enter the cave and you will find yourself walking for hours through chambers with walls that vanish into shadows. Stalactites of quartz descend from the ceilings and veins of jade run along the walls like rivers. The air is fresh, like mountain air after a storm. Time folds, stretches, and sometimes disappears.

To enter the cave is to enter not just inward, but downward into a depth where boundaries dissolve. Here, there are no speakers. No listeners. You are only present. Unlike the passive presence of observation this is an active presence engaging fully with what arises. Bring this quality of attentive presence to difficult conversations and you will discover that you and the other can remain without pressure to defend, persuade, or retreat. This presence is experienced as a joint field; as an invitation to meet in a space beyond fixed positions. The blue dragon dwells in this space of shared presence. Here boundaries between self and other dissolve and a new understanding emerges.

Some years ago, a young monk approached me, proposing that our monastery should not rely on silence to attract newcomers. "People must know we are here," he said. "We must use all means possible: signs, stories, and strategy." His language was shaped by the world beyond our walls. Words such as visibility, outreach, and engagement came easily to him. I listened and felt the ancient stone within me resist.

I had grown old with the idea that those who truly seek the Way will find it. Not because we call them, but because they are already listening. To announce ourselves seemed to me like shouting during meditation.

I said little. Over the days that followed, I asked questions. Not to direct him away from his path, but to walk with him a little while upon it. What, I wondered, had made him speak with such urgency?

And so, he told me about the people he met while traveling. Young people, uncertain and unrooted. He spoke of a world so loud that there could be no silence. "They are searching," he said, "but don't know for what. And they won't find it if we are concealed behind the quiet isolation of the Temple."

I did not agree. But I understood. And in that understanding, a subtle change took place.

We made no proclamation. There were no slogans. But a few paths were cleared a little further out. A small bell was placed beside the gate and lights were added.

Not compromise, but attentiveness. Not concession, but inclusion.

Another time, I sat across from a city developer who hoped to build luxury residences near the temple's outer grove. His language, too, came dressed in numbers: square footage, projected yield, environmental offsets.

My heart resisted. I thought only of the cedar roots we had never disturbed, of the deer who passed each spring, the silence that gathers beneath those trees like water in a deep well.

And yet again, I said little. Then I asked him, "What brought you to this work?"

His answer surprised me.

He spoke of a childhood in buildings in which residents did not know their neighbors. Of hallways echoing with footsteps but never greetings. "I want to build places," he said, "where people can live without feeling alone."

His voice lowered as he spoke. He was no longer presenting a plan. He was experiencing a longing.

We did not agree. The construction never occurred. But we parted with bows and appropriate formalities.

The blue dragon dwells in these points in time as a presence that arrives when certainty diminishes. In its cave, disagreement does not produce conflict. Therefore, the dragon has no resolution to pursue. Oppositions are perceived as a totality, like waves rising from the same ocean.

You ask how to respond when the other side clings to views that seem misguided or even harmful. You wonder how to listen without agreeing, how to hold your ground without creating an enemy.

The answer is not a technique. It is a way of being.

Release the grip of needing to be understood. Dull the edge of needing to win. Let silence speak longer than usual.

In that quiet you may hear what was hidden. A fear behind a demand. A longing behind a position. An origin story inside an opinion.

You do not need to agree to understand. You do not need to yield to ease.

Sometimes, even in disagreement, the field between you changes. Sometimes, it does not.

But when you return from the dragon's cave, a part of you remains a little tranquil, a little more open. The need to classify, defend, or prove no longer presses so hard.

The Familiar Stranger
When Certainty Dissolves

The moon cast faint silhouettes of the stone lanterns. I had risen long before dawn to sweep the path to the zendo. It was my solitary walking meditation. In the dim light of the gibbous moon, I could see the dew covered ground. I listened to the movement of branches in the breeze and the murmur of the stream near the wall. There was the distant call of a night heron.

Then, I saw him. He was standing beside the ancient pine. His way of standing was exactly as I remembered from the few early childhood memories I carried: tall, straight shoulders, arms behind his back. I saw the same strength and dignity I recalled from childhood. The lines in his face expressed the patient endurance of a lifetime as a fisherman.

My father.

I froze and gazed at him silently thinking, Why now, after eighty years?

His voice seemed to come from within me rather than from the moonlit apparition.

"You came back to her," he said.

"Yes," I replied. "When she was ninety-two."

"She spoke of your visit often in her final years," he continued. "How you helped restore the garden's water channels. How you listened to her guidance before acting."

The memory surfaced: Obaachan directing from her bench, my careful attention to her every instruction. But now another memory arose alongside it: how deliberate my attention had been, how conscious my every movement. Had I been present with her, or performing presence to alleviate my own guilt?

"I know that I should have returned sooner," I said, the words emerging without emotional charge, although a quiet undercurrent of uncertainty stirred beneath them.

"You returned to her when you were most needed."

"Most needed by whom? Did I visit when my need was greatest or hers? Was I rationalizing my belief that I had not abandoned her?"

"Our actions are driven by many motivations," he replied. "She had no bitterness that you had not visited in twenty years." She understood. 'The mountain called him,' she would often say.

"It was convenient for me to believe that the mountain called me. Was this not an excuse to justify abandoning an old woman when she most required my care?"

"The path demands total commitment."

"Yes," he agreed. "She understood this."

But did I understand it? Perhaps my commitment to the dharma had not been renunciation? Maybe it was an elaborate escape. Had I chosen the path to realization, or had I fled from the complications and struggles of human obligation?

"During that last visit," my father continued, "she saw in you a quality of attention she had not seen before. She said you listened to the plants, to the stones, to the flow of water."

I remembered this clearly, the quiet focus I had brought to each task, the way I had moved through the garden as if in meditation. But now I wondered: Was that presence, or performance? Was I serving her, or serving my image of myself as someone who serves?

The self-inquiry was relentless now, each memory examined with the precision I had once applied to observing breath. I watched myself watching her, noted how conscious I had been of my own awareness, how aware of being the dutiful grandson returned.

"When you worked beside her," he said, "she told the neighbors, 'He has brought back more than ideas from the mountain. What he knows now lives not only in his mind, but in his hands.'"

Had I found insight, or had I learned to imitate learning? The question cut deeper than any external accusation. After decades of sitting, of studying emptiness and non-self, was I any different from the seven-year-old boy who had fled his grief into the care of patient grand-parents?

I felt the uncertain ground of my understanding, like sand redistrib-uting under slowly moving water. Not dramatically, not with panic, but with the recognition that what I had taken for spiritual accomplish-ment was more complex than I had allowed myself to see.

"She died peacefully," he said. "Two years after your visit. In her final weeks, she would sit in the garden and speak of the water's voice returning."

The water's voice. I had cleared those channels with such careful attention, such reverence for the task. But even that memory now felt suspect. Had I been present to the water, or to my own nobility in serving?

"You carry a weight that troubles you," my father observed, although his tone held no judgment.

"I carry doubt about the authenticity of my path."

My admission emerged with startling clarity. Not as confession, but as recognition of what had been gathering beneath conscious awareness for years.

"When I returned to help her," I continued, "I was offering presence. Now I wonder if I was performing presence to convince myself I had not become completely selfish."

He listened without attempting to reassure or correct.

"For sixty years," I said, "I have practiced letting go of self. But per-haps the process of letting go of the self was just one more illusion. Pursuing this path was a justification for abandoning the people who needed me."

My words hung in the morning air. I observed how speaking them brought neither relief nor increased distress, only a quality of naked-ness. I stood there in the moonlight without the familiar supports of identity or achievement.

"These questions," my father said finally, "do they serve awakening or suffering?"

"They serve truth," I said. "Does truth serve awakening?"

Rather than defending against uncertainty, I found myself meeting it with the same quality of attention I reserved for breath.

"She loved you as you were," he said. "Not as the unrealized ideal of a devoted grandson, but as the boy who listened to her stories."

A quietness settled in my chest. It was not resolution but a different kind of space. I realized that to question everything, including the questioner, was itself a form of presence.

"Has my practice been authentic?" I asked. "Is realization itself a final illusion?

I sensed rather than saw the same gentle expression I remembered from childhood.

"Authentic practice begins with authentic doubt," he replied. "Continue questioning. But question with presence, not with anguish. Let uncertainty become a doorway rather than a wall."

As the sun approached the horizon, his form seemed to blend with the rose light. And then was gone. The bell rang for morning meditation.

As I walked to the zendo, the questions remained. Questions about authenticity and spiritual awakening. But they were held now in awareness that no longer needed answers to remain present.

My practice continued. But what had been the practice of a realized monk was now the practice of a beginner. And somewhere in the space between doubt and certainty, presence revealed itself as that which required no justification.

The Wisdom and the Shadow
The Weight of Unspoken Truth

Ten years ago, I was invited to speak at a peace conference in Hiroshima. It was held at the International Conference Center in Hiroshima Peace Memorial Park in an auditorium with seating for eight hundred. I was asked to speak on the subject, "Zen and the Cultivation of Peace."

There were five speakers seated on the stage facing a crowded audience. Many people were standing at the back and in the aisles. I was scheduled last. I listened to diplomats and professors choose their words carefully. I felt the energy of evocative issues as history and hope wove themselves together in formal language.

When my name was introduced, I walked to the podium and for an instant questioned the legitimacy of my attendance at this gathering. On what authority, on what experiential knowledge could I offer words of meaning to the hundreds of expectant faces?

I bowed once to the room and began.

I spoke about Buddha's teachings that hatred can only be quenched by loving kindness. I referred to Dogen's emphasis on *shikantaza*, just sitting, as a practice that vanquishes the impulses that lead to violence. I quoted Huang Po on the pure mind for which there are no boundaries between self and other.

These were familiar phrases used often in my decades of teaching. But here, in this city, they seemed to hover just above a depth I could sense but not name.

"I accepted the invitation to be here today to speak about peace, but frankly, I do not know what peace is. I can say what peace is not. It is not an objective. It is not a goal. It is not the absence of conflict that occurs when adversaries are muted.

"Peace is the disappearance of our need to be right and our fear of being wrong. Peace is the exhalation that returns when we let go.

"Zen teaches that the separation between self and other is an illusion. The suffering of one is the suffering of all. When we harm another, we harm ourselves. When we heal another, we heal ourselves. Peace is not an inaccessible place. It is the path you follow in anger or with openness."

I looked at the faces in the room. Many stared at me with steady gaze and inscrutable expression. In the third row, an elderly Japanese woman sat with her hands folded, her face a map of lines. In the front row a young woman typed on her tablet.

"Peace is the recognition that there is no one outside the circle of our care. I bow to the soldier and to the victim, to the one who gives orders and the one who obeys them. All are caught in the web of causes and conditions."

As I spoke, my doubts multiplied. Were my words an incomplete truth? I did not know how to find the right language to convey that conflict arises from attachment. And attachment leads only to suffering.

"I do not offer guiding principles. Peace is not won by force, by argument, or by clinging to our stories. It is found in the tranquility that remains when the stories fall away."

In the momentary hush I thought of this conference center built near what had been the hypocenter seventy years ago. The instant of quiet was broken by fifteen seconds of applause. The moderator thanked me with customary polite formality and invited the audience to ask questions.

A middle-aged woman, dressed in a dark blue skirt and white blouse, stepped up to the microphone.

"I would like to direct this question to the Roshi."

I inclined my head and focused on her completely.

"Your talk was eloquent," she began, and I heard the "but" coming before she spoke it.

"But I am disturbed by what you did not discuss. How can you reconcile these Zen Buddhist teachings of compassion with the historical reality that the most prominent Zen masters in Japan supported Japanese imperialism?"

She directed a cold stare at me and then continued. "Those Zen masters taught that killing for the emperor was a form of Buddhist practice. They promoted the idea that Japanese people are superior to other Asians.

"Prominent Zen masters, including Daisetz Teitaro Suzuki, whose many books introduced Zen to the West, Yasutani Haku'un Rōshi, and Kōdō Sawaki Rōshi quoted Zen teachings to support Japan's military aggression. They referred to *yamato-damashii*, the 'Japanese spirit,' as the highest principle. They said that loyalty to the emperor was an expression of Buddhist enlightenment. Their term, 'Imperial-Way Zen,' replaced 'Buddha-Way Zen' in their dharma talks, in their public statements, and in their writings. They taught that selflessness meant dying for the emperor, that obedience to the state was the highest form of Zen practice. They said that Japanese military supremacy was an extension of Buddha's teachings."

The room was absolutely hushed. It was hushed in a way that felt quite different from the respectful quiet during my talk. It was the muteness of held air. I felt the pressure of every gaze, the way the atmosphere itself seemed to thicken with an uneasy expectancy.

I inhaled once, feeling my feet on the floor, the weight of my body, the sensation of standing in this particular instant in this particular room with this particular question suspended in the air between us.

"Yasutani Roshi," she continued, "wrote that killing in war is an expression of compassion. Sawaki Roshi asserted that all Japanese people must be prepared to die for the emperor. Those who made these claims were among the most revered teachers of modern Zen."

She hesitated, and in that interval I saw in her eyes pain and anger.

"How can we respect a tradition that not only failed to prevent such delusion but actively promoted it? Where was the wisdom? Where was the compassion for the millions who suffered and died?"

I took a deep inhalation and slowly exhaled. I stood with what she had given me. I let quiet fill the space between us -- her words, her pain, her challenge. I let them settle without trying to reshape them into a form easier to bear. "You are right to ask these questions," I said. "And you are right to be troubled by what I didn't say."

I let her words settle and stepped away from the podium, closer to where she stood. The movement felt necessary, as if the formal distance of the stage had become an obstacle to communication.

"The history you describe is accurate. It is shameful." I halted, feeling the weight of those words, the way they seemed to echo in the space between us. "And I don't know what to do with it."

The woman's expression changed; perhaps she was not expecting my frankness. I saw surprise and relief, as if she had been prepared for evasion and was grateful not to encounter it.

I looked at her completely and inhaled once deliberately. "Those teachers were our lineage holders. They used the teachings I discussed earlier to justify killing. I stand here in the same robes, carrying their transmission, and I do not know how to reconcile that."

The room was completely quiet. I could hear the faint hum of the air conditioning, the distant sound of traffic from the street below, but these seemed to come from another world.

"You ask about legitimacy. I ask myself that question every day."

I looked directly at her, trying to meet not just her eyes but the pain behind them.

"How can I teach about compassion when my tradition blessed soldiers going to war? How can I speak of no-separation when my predecessors taught that Japanese people were spiritually superior?"

For a long interval, I did not continue. Finally, I said, "I don't believe that there can be an answer that resolves this contradiction."

An older Japanese man approached the microphone. He moved carefully, with the thoughtful dignity of someone carrying an invisible burden. His face was weathered, his hair white.

"I was a child during the war," he said. "My father and uncle died in the Philippines believing they were serving the Buddha by serving the emperor. How can I, or anyone, trust the Zen tradition?"

I let his words sink into me completely. His father. His uncle. Men who had died believing they were serving realization while serving empire. The weight of that betrayal, not just of the men who died, but of this man who had carried their memory for a lifetime.

"Your father deserved better teachers than mine. Your father and uncle were betrayed," I said. "By teachers who should have known better. By a tradition that should have protected them from such delusion, not encouraged it."

I bowed toward him to express what language could not.

"I cannot imagine carrying that pain," I continued. "The knowledge that the people you loved died for a lie wrapped in sacred terminology."

I saw in his face the weight of decades, the burden of loving people who had been fundamentally misled by those they trusted most.

"I don't see how you could trust this tradition," I said. "And perhaps no one can. I do know that I try to practice in a way that doesn't repeat those mistakes."

"What would you say to my father if you could meet him?" the man asked.

I was quiet for a long time, feeling the question move through me. What would I say to a man who had died convinced that killing for the emperor was Buddhist practice? Were there words that could bridge the betrayal?

"I would say," I replied, "that he deserved teachers who would have told him that killing in service of empire is not compassion. It is violence. I would tell him that his practice was misled by people who confused nationalism with realization."

I very slowly inhaled and exhaled.

"I would tell him that his sincerity mattered, even though it was misdirected. That the longing for truth that brought him to Zen was worthy."

"And to the victims of that violence?" he asked.

"That their deaths mattered. That the teachings used to justify their killing were wrong. And I cannot say that carrying this tradition forward honors them or continues to betray them."

The admission hung in the air between us. I had never spoken it aloud before, though it had lived in me for years. The fundamental uncertainty about whether continuing the tradition was an act of heal-ing or of perpetuation.

"So why do you continue? Why not abandon a tradition so com-promised?"

"I see your need for an answer," I said. "I don't have one that serves you. If I carry this tradition, I have to carry its shadows too. Maybe that's what practice means now, sitting with the unbearable knowledge of what we're capable of when we stop questioning ourselves."

"That doesn't sound like much of an answer," he said.

"It is not," I agreed. "It is just staying with the question. Even when there's no good answer."

I looked around the room, seeing faces that reflected confusion, pain, disappointment. Some had come expecting wisdom or clarity. Instead, they were witnessing uncertainty, brokenness, the admission that the tradition they might have looked to for guidance had once been fundamentally compromised.

"Maybe uncertainty is all I have to offer," I continued. "Not confi-dence that Zen prevents suffering. It does not. Only the willingness to continue asking: What harm am I causing right now that I can't see? What am I so certain about that I've stopped questioning it?"

A movement in the front row captured my attention. The elderly Japanese woman I had noticed earlier was rising deliberately. She moved with determined exertion. Both hands rested on the back of the chair in front of her. When she spoke, her tranquil tone and simple words carried the authority of lived experience.

"I am a *hibakusha*. I am a survivor. I was in Hiroshima when the bomb fell," she said, her voice thin but clear. "We lived in Hesaka about five kilometers from the hypocenter. We were far enough to survive the blast, but close enough to see the sky go white. I was twelve years old."

Her words pressed against the walls of the silent hall, against our chests, against the invisible barriers we had unconsciously built around the conversation.

"I have spent my life trying to understand how people could do such things to one another. Not only the Americans who dropped the bomb, but also our own leaders who led us into that war. The teachers.

The officials. They were the ones we trusted to protect us. I remember how we were taught to believe, to obey. And then they disappeared."

She looked directly at me, and I felt the full force of her gaze.

"You say you don't know. You say you're uncertain. But you're wearing those robes. You're teaching. Why do you continue when you admit you could be perpetuating the same delusions?"

I stood with her question for a long time, feeling it work its way through me. What did give me the right to continue? What gave any of us the right to carry forward traditions that had proven capable of such terrible distortion?

"I don't think I have that right," I said finally. "I don't think any of us do. But I also don't think we have the right to abandon it."

I looked at her, this woman who had lived through unimaginable trauma, who had spent a lifetime grappling with questions that had no answers. I heard the anguish in her tone.

"Maybe continuing isn't about having the right. Maybe it's about accepting the responsibility. The responsibility to carry both the wisdom and the shadow, to hold both the beauty and the horror, and to keep asking whether we're adding to the healing or the harm."

"And how will you know?" she asked.

I was quiet for an extended interval. "I cannot know," I said.

She looked at me thoughtfully and then walked away from the microphone.

I felt a current pass between us in that exchange. It was not agreement, but a shared recognition of the weight we were all holding.

The moderator glanced at her watch and offered some concluding comments. People gathered their things and began moving toward the exits.

The woman who had asked the first question approached me as I stepped down from the small platform. "Thank you," she said. "For not defending what is indefensible."

She hesitated, studying my face. "Do you believe that Zen practice today can prevent this from happening again?"

I was quiet for an interval, feeling the weight of the question one more time.

"I don't know," I said. "I hope that living day-to-day with these questions will help."

As I walked back to my hotel through the streets of Hiroshima, I thought about the cracked bronze bell hanging in our monastery tower. How its broken voice had taught us to listen differently, to find what was always there beneath our expectations of how things should sound.

The tradition I carried was also cracked. Its voice had been distorted by historical complicity. But perhaps that brokenness offered an essential message: Practice without constant self-questioning becomes spiritual delusion. The instant we believe that we are beyond causing harm, we become capable of great harm.

The streets around me held their own historical burden, as though the earth itself carried the memory of what had happened here. And yet life continued. People had chosen to go on, had rebuilt and found ways to carry both trauma and hope.

I passed a small shrine wedged between two tall office buildings, its wooden structure dark with age. Someone had left fresh flowers, bright against the weathered wood. I stopped and bowed. I bowed to the recognition that some forms of care persist despite the worst adversity.

People continue to tend to what matters even in the face of overwhelming uncertainty. We must be willing to embrace the question of how to live without causing suffering, even when the answer accuses us.

I bowed toward the city around me, to all those who had suffered, to all those who had caused suffering while believing they served a greater cause.

Perhaps it is enough to remain aware of the possibility that we are making the same mistakes again in ways we cannot see.

The broken bell in the monastery would continue to ring its fractured song, calling us to the endless practice of beginning again with humility and the willingness to be wrong about everything we thought we knew.

We must remain with the question: How do we live without causing harm? This is presence. It is taking the next step, even when there is no path to follow.

Conclusion
The Way Is Everywhere and Nowhere

The path winds down now, though endings and beginnings are often a matter of perspective. What finishes here continues somewhere else: in the breath you take, in the pause before your next conversation, in the quiet interval between one difficulty and another.

We have walked together through many places -- hospital rooms and temple gardens, train stations and city streets, kitchens where tempers flared and parks where strangers paused to speak. In every place, the same invitation appeared, to be present with whatever arose.

The monk who swept a courtyard, the woman who drank her tea, they each dwelled in the fleeting instant they were given. You possess this ability. In the next heated moment, in the space where you can choose between defending and staying open, presence waits.

Many of the stories left questions unanswered, doors unopened, wounds unhealed. Presence does not promise a perfect ending. It offers instead the capacity to meet whatever comes with an open heart.

As you close this book, what remains? Ideas? Stories? Or the awareness that has been reading these words? That awareness is the Way. It needs only to be noticed, like an old friend waiting patiently at the door while you looked everywhere else.

When conflict returns do not forget: you are not broken, the other person is not your enemy. The situation is not a problem to solve. It is an opportunity to meet. In that meeting the Way reveals itself.

There is no graduation from this practice, no final mastery. Each conversation is fresh. Each misunderstanding an invitation. Each heated moment a doorway back to presence.

The tea cools. The light shifts across the floor. Footsteps echo down the hall. All of it, change and continuity, harmony and conflict, words and emptiness, arises within the same serene presence. You have always been this presence.

The Way is not a path. There is no path. There is no destination. There is only the capacity to be here. Like the mountain holding the storm. Like the sky holding the clouds. Like the silence holding every word. Always here. Always now.

Glossary of Terms

Abbot (*Jūshoku*) – The head priest or chief administrator of a Buddhist monastery

Attachment – Clinging to people, things, or ideas, which Buddhism sees as causing suffering

Bafun uni – Type of sea urchin prized in Japanese cuisine for its deep umami flavor.

Bell – Used in Buddhist temples/ceremonies to mark periods, transitions, or meditation sessions

Bochi – A small cemetery, typically located on temple grounds

Bosalsang – Korean term for a bodhisattva statue

Compassion – Active concern for the suffering of others

Cultural Revolution – Political upheaval in China (1966-1976) that suppressed religious practices

Dharma – The teachings of the Buddha; universal truth or natural law

Dōgen (1200-1253) – Founder of Sōtō Zen in Japan, author of the *Shōbōgenzō*

Eiheiji – One of the two head temples of Sōtō Zen Buddhism in Japan

Emptiness (*Śūnyatā*) – The Buddhist teaching that all phenomena lack inherent existence

Enzu – The monk responsible for managing the temple's vegetable garden

Equanimity – Mental calmness and composure in difficult situations

Fusu – The temple treasurer responsible for financial matters

Ghost boat – Drifting boats from North Korea found off the coast of Japan

Greater East Asia War – Japanese term for their involvement in World War II

Heart Sutra – A fundamental Buddhist text on the nature of emptiness

Hibakusha – Japanese term for survivors of the atomic bombings of Hiroshima and Nagasaki

Hesaka – A district in Hiroshima mentioned in the hibakusha's testimony

Ichi-go ichi-e – "One time, one meeting" – the principle that each encounter is unique

Imperial-Way Zen – A militarized reinterpretation of Zen aligned with ultranationalist ideologies during wartime Japan

Impermanence (*Anicca*) – The Buddhist teaching that all things are transient

Incense – Burned during meditation and ceremonies as an offering

Jikijitsu – The monk who maintains order and timing during meditation periods

Jizō – A bodhisattva in Japanese Buddhism, protector of travelers and children

Kaimyō – A posthumous Buddhist name given to the deceased

Kalyāṇa-mitta – Sanskrit term for "noble friend" or spiritual companion

Katsujinken – "The sword that gives life" – words or actions that awaken rather than harm

Kioke – Traditional Japanese wooden barrels used for fermenting soy sauce

Kumonryu – A variety of koi fish known for its black-and-white patterning that resembles ink brush strokes or a dragon moving through clouds

Letting go – Releasing attachment to outcomes, people, or fixed ideas

Lineage – The transmission of teachings from master to student across generations

Ma (間) – The meaningful space, pause, or interval between things

Maki-wari – The practice of splitting firewood, often assigned to novice monks

Meditation hall – See *zendo*

Mindfulness – Awareness of present-moment experience without judgment

Miso shiru – Traditional Japanese soup made with fermented soybean paste

Non-attachment – Engaging fully without clinging to results

Non-self (*Anattā*) – The Buddhist teaching that there is no fixed, permanent self

Obaachan – Informal term for grandmother

Occupation – Allied occupation of Japan (1945-1952) following World War II

Ojiichan – Informal term for grandfather

Presence – Complete attention to the current moment without judgment or agenda

Public Security Bureau – China's primary domestic security agency

Realization – Direct understanding of Buddhist truths through practice

Roshi – An honorific title for a Zen master or senior teacher

Satsujinken – "The sword that kills" – words or actions that harm or divide

Shakkin – Debt or financial obligation

Shikibuton – A thin Japanese futon mattress used for sleeping

Shikantaza – "Just sitting" – a form of Zen meditation without focused concentration

Shobadai – Protection money or tribute paid to organized crime groups

Shōbōgenzō – "Treasury of the True Dharma Eye," Dōgen's masterwork on Zen philosophy

Shoji – A traditional sliding door, window, or room divider made of a wooden lattice frame.

Sitting meditation – See *zazen*

Sōgi – A Buddhist funeral ritual

Stillness – Inner calm that remains steady regardless of external circumstances

Stone garden – Zen garden using rocks and gravel to represent natural landscapes

Sutra – A Buddhist scripture containing the teachings of the Buddha

Tiantong Temple – The Chinese temple mentioned in "The Jade Pendant"

Two Arrows – Buddha's teaching distinguishing unavoidable pain from self-created suffering

Walking meditation – Slow, mindful walking as a form of meditation practice

Washi – Traditional Japanese paper made from plant fibers

Wu-wei – Taoist principle of effortless action or non-interference

Yakusoku yaburi – Breaking promises or failing to honor commitments

Yamato-damashii – A concept of the "Japanese spirit," often invoked in wartime rhetoric to promote national unity and sacrifice

Zazen – Seated meditation practice in Zen Buddhism

Zendo – The meditation hall in a Zen monastery

Zuhatsu – A black lacquerware bowl used by monks for meals